<u>Observations of a Planner</u>

THE
Quest

FOR
FINANCIAL INDEPENDENCE

10 Areas of Your Planning You Should Not Ignore

Stanley T. Funches

CFP®, ChFC®, CRPC®, MBA

Published in the United States by INTELUS Wealth Management, LLC.
www.inteluswm.com

Funches, Stanley T.
The quest for financial independence : 10 areas of your planning you should not ignore / Stanley T. Funches.
pages   cm
ISBN 978–1–7333604–0–1 (pbk)
ISBN 978–1–7333604–1–8 (ebook)
1. Finance, Personal. 2. Retirement income—Planning. 3. Early retirement.
I. Author. II. Title.

Edited by Christopher J. Levin

Printed in the United States of America
First Printing, 2019

Acknowledgements

I am a product of all the wonderful people who have been a part of my life and this journey thus far.

I would like to say thank you *to:*

God, for his many blessings. He is ever-present in my life and He is the source for all that is good.

My father, Solon Funches, for his many lessons and instilling a sense of family and discipline. You have always made me feel like I could accomplish anything.

My mother, Hazel Funches, for teaching me love and what it truly means to sacrifice for the ones you love.

My children, Ashli, TJ, and Christopher, for being my inspiration for all that I do, being good kids, and bringing true joy to my life

Dee, for being a great daughter to our parents and a supportive little sister.

Aunts, uncles and cousins, for being a family that's always there to show love.

Venessa, without our journey together, I would not have achieved this level of success in this industry nor had the opportunity to write this book. Many great things came from our time together. Thank you!

Janelle, for being the best practice manager that I could ever ask for!

Rico and Bryan, for being great brothers from another mother. Love you both!

"Joe," for your support, companionship and laughs!

My Counselor, for your friendship, support, and encouragement. Your presence helped me stay strong and prosper through a difficult time.

To all of my clients who have allowed me to serve them in their quest for financial independence!

Table of Contents

Introduction

Welcome to *The Quest for Financial Independence: 10 Areas of Your Planning You Should Not Ignore*, the first book in the **Observations of a Planner** series.

If you're reading this, you have a goal in mind: achieving financial independence. You know you want to reach a stage in life when you no longer need to work and when you can live the life you want to live comfortably.

I'm here to help you pursue that goal.

Like many of my clients, you may be wondering how you compare to others, where you stand now financially, and whether you are on track to meet your own goals and dreams of financial independence.

This book can tell you. It can provide a roadmap to financial independence, help you determine your current waypoint, and guide you along your route to the end. It will teach you what you need to focus on to stay on track, no matter your stage of life.

The 10 areas of planning and wealth creation covered here are informed by the firsthand observations of a financial planner with decades of experience helping countless clients plan for and maintain their financial independence. They have been demonstrated time and time again.

And for them to work for you, you need one thing: initiative. You've shown you have it by picking up this book.

You're ready to educate yourself on financial planning and the principles of wealth creation. This is your time. And this is your book. This book is for everybody who is ready to take the next step: setting your sights on a goal and seeing how far your determination can take you.

We All Have Dreams

As I write this introduction, I think about my own walk and how far I've come. Currently, my daughter is in college studying to become an actor. I often tell her of the time when a now well-respected and well-accomplished movie director and producer slept on her mom and dad's floor. She has heard this story ad nauseam, but retelling it still produces in me both a sense of amazement in how blessed and successful friends and acquaintances have become by pursuing their dreams.

We all have dreams. And there's no telling where they can take you if you put your mind to it. One of my dreams was to be a financial planner, to help people work toward their own dreams and financial goals. But another one of my dreams was to one day write a book. I remember, those 20-some years ago, when that director and his then-fiancé came to visit for the weekend.

At that time, I was a young middle-level manager at a company, just out of college and newly married. I had earned my degree in finance, and investments were one of my favorite things. I was always talking to people at work about investing. However, I wasn't yet in the financial planning business. At that point, I was an avid reader, and I had just finished Kelvin Boston's classic *Smart Money Moves for African-Americans*. It was a great book for me at the time.

That weekend, we had visitors. One of our family friends, who was studying to be a doctor, was in town with her film-buff fiancé. We rolled out the welcome mat and the sleeping bags. Our friends saw *Smart Money Moves* lying on the coffee table and asked, "Hey! Have you finished reading this book?" "Yeah, I just finished it. You guys can take it," I offered. And they did. Although they did not wed, each one of them did go on to have extremely successful careers following their aspirations. Sometimes I wonder what impact that book had in their financial lives. But for me, the moment they enthusiastically took that book had another meaning.

At that moment, I had a dream of writing a book that people would look at the same way our friends had looked at Kelvin Boston's *Smart Money Moves*. I dreamed of having a book that people would want to read to help better their lives, that sparked that same enthusiasm and excitement for financial knowledge that our friends got as they read it as young people.

Many years later, I think about how at that time, all of us were aspiring to do something different with our lives. We all took our own paths to get there. I'm certainly nowhere near the level of being a famous filmmaker, and yet I have achieved many of the dreams that I set out to accomplish from that pivotal moment. I took my passion for educating people and turned it into a successful career as a financial planner, where I continue to be inspired by the faith, joy, and perseverance of my clients. And I have taken that dream of writing a book and turned it into *The Quest for Financial Independence: 10 Areas of Your Planning You Should Not Ignore*.

This Book Is for You if...

In life, we sometimes have those "aha" moments where you realize that you want to write a book, or you want to start a business, or you want to retire early and travel. My hope is that this book will help you articulate those "aha" moments that you need to help set your goals, and will also teach you what you need to know, where you need to take action, and where you need to focus in order to make them your reality.

This book is for you, whether you are just starting to think about saving and investing or you're already planning for your future financial independence. It's also for those of you who are already retired, as it will help to guide your decisions in this stage of life. However, this book is not Personal Finance 101, nor is it a get-out-of-debt book. Those are important topics, but not the focus of these pages. Instead, this book looks at 10 common and not-so-common aspects of financial health from a viewpoint you may not have read before: the view of this planner.

From the Planner's Perspective

Financial planners help millions of Americans, from the employee to the small-business owner and the uber-rich entrepreneur, budget, save, invest, and manage their assets. As financial planners, we are there during the boom times and the dot-com busts, the Great Recessions and their recoveries. We see a very personal side of our clients, during their highs and their lows, both financially as well as emotionally. All of this gives financial planners a unique perspective on finance as well as life.

In this book, I try to give you a different way of thinking about financial topics such as expenses, savings, asset types, volatility, and more. This book also delves into topics that are incredibly important on your path to financial independence but that are often underrated or even ignored as parts of that journey, like family, marriage, health, and finding peace.

In financial planning, the choices you make now affect your future probability of success, whether the choice is buying a bigger house or having an extra slice of pizza. This book looks at wealth creation, wealth maintenance, financial independence, and legacy planning from a new, holistic perspective. I hope you enjoy it. I hope you learn something. And I wish you success as you take your next step toward gaining financial independence and living the life you want to live.

THE
Quest
FOR
FINANCIAL INDEPENDENCE

10 Areas of Your Planning You Should Not Ignore

Chapter 1: The Vision

As we begin, it is important to note that many factors work together to help build up your money, and every one of them is important. I'll touch on them all, but before we start, we need a unifying purpose. As business author Stephen Covey discusses in his book *The 7 Habits of Highly Effective People*, you should begin with the end in mind. For financial planning, this means that we need to start with a vision.

I remember how my grade school teachers used to tell us to set goals. As a kid growing up in Clinton, Mississippi, I knew from a very early age I wanted to go to a college with high academic standards and a great reputation. That was my goal and my vision. I didn't know exactly how I was going to do it at first, but I realized that keeping my grades up was the first step to make my vision a reality. So, I made sure I did.

Years later, I graduated from the type of college I envisioned, and then I began my professional career. Like many people, I began to settle into a routine, thinking more about the next little step, the next raise or promotion, and less about the bigger vision.

It was around this time that I read Stephen Covey's *7 Habits* for the first time, and his first piece of advice was to begin with the end in mind. That guidance transformed my way of thinking by reinforcing that goal-oriented way of thinking I had when I was a kid and had lost over the years. In the decades since I restructured my thinking and decision-making around that goal-focused mindset, I've continued to use this mindset in many areas of life, including financial planning.

What Is Your Vision of Financial Independence?

It is important to paint a picture for yourself of what you want your life to look like in your career, in your personal life, and in your financial independence and retirement. As my teachers used to ask, "What is your goal?"

As a planner, I try to help clients define their vision of financial independence. Ask yourself what you would like to have the ability to do and how you would like your life to look. Eventually, you will need to get to what it's going to cost to gain the level of financial independence where your money does all the work for you and you can retire comfortably. But to start, ask yourself what that picture looks like for you.

You may think about things that you've never thought about before. Some people realize they have conflicting desires. They may not want to stop working because they enjoy what they're doing, but at the same time they want to have the option. Others may be torn between owning a large home and downsizing so they can travel more. Whatever your financial goals, you should try to crystallize what that vision looks like, what it is going to cost you, and what your roadmap will be to achieve your goal. In my experience, these are the three most important questions to ask yourself as you articulate your vision:

- What does a day look like?
- What do you enjoy?
- Who will you serve?

What Does a Day Look Like?

Imagine your future self. You have achieved your financial independence and you no longer have the obligation of employment. Think about your vision of what a typical day looks like for you.

Visualize getting up in the morning. Let's say it's a Wednesday. You have no place you need to be. Do you have a morning coffee? Take a morning walk? Spend time at the gym? What are your favorite activities and how do you fill your day with them?

The psychology of going through this exercise as you prepare for financial independence is powerful. I've met people who have this vision clearly defined for themselves years before they make the decision to become financially independent. I have also met others who hadn't given it much thought. Either way, the best time to think about the future is the present, especially as you are beginning to build towards your long-term goals.

What Do You Enjoy?

As your future self is going about your day, what are those favorite activities you are spending your time doing? Imagine that you are truly financially free, where on a day-to-day basis you can do the reasonable majority of things that you would like to do, and that your money is doing it for you. Travel, charity work, and spending time with the grandchildren are a few of the activities which may come to mind. Or you may picture yourself just living a comfortable lifestyle.

Whatever your vision, I can tell you it is extremely important to keep up your activity. Many people think about retiring *from* something, but it's also important to have something to retire *to*. Having something to retire to will not only motivate you to prepare properly for financial independence, it will also help keep you healthier and happier while in retirement.

If your plan is to travel — a popular and very fulfilling goal — try outlining some key destinations and telling others about your specific plans. In one case, one of my clients, a teacher, dreamed of a trip to Alaska. I watched as her determination and motivation helped her make great decisions as she worked toward her financial independence and toward that specific goal. She was motivated. It was a great experience for her when she finally was able to travel there. Whatever your destination, having these personalized dreams which you will retire *to* will help hold you accountable to your life goals while giving you something to work toward.

Who Will You Serve?

As you picture your own personal vision of financial independence, you will likely think about others in your life. Your partner, your children and grandchildren, your friends, your community. It is only natural that the people who are important in your life now will also be a part of your future.

I often hear clients discuss who they will serve once their careers are complete. Many want to leave a legacy for their grandchildren. Not just with money, but with actions. Spending time with their grandchildren, teaching them life lessons, and creating memories with travel. I have had others tell me about their commitment to church or special charities. And I have known quite a few who leave the workforce to take care of an ailing parent or spouse.

These are an important part of your vision, because I believe there is no greater purpose in life than what we do for others. In the end, that is all that matters. I have often observed that striving to reach a financial goal in order to serve others and contribute to something bigger than themselves can be some clients' greatest motivation.

What Will You Retire *to*?

I have found that a client's own motivation for achieving financial independence can be just as important as developing the financial discipline needed to save and prepare for life after work. Not developing that motivation can lead people to miss the mark on articulating and executing a solid vision.

A common mistake that leads to fuzzy goals and a lack of motivation is not considering a retirement vision beyond just an age. "I want to stop working at 55." Or "I want to retire at 70." These clients don't develop other goals to pursue in all the years to come after that point. Others are eager to leave the workforce. "I am so ready to leave this job." Or "I'm tired, and I can't do this anymore." These people are typically ready to retire *from* something. Yet, they have no idea of what they are retiring *to*. Other people believe they have to stop being active to conform to what society says retirement is. These people may consider themselves a failure if they want or need to continue working. For these reasons, many retire when they are not ready.

As you imagine your vision of what you will retire to, consider whether you will still need the challenges and interactions with others that your current work life provides in order to feel fulfilled. There is absolutely no shame in continuing to work if that's what you desire.

CONTINUING TO WORK LATER IN LIFE

MILLIONS OF SENIORS CONTINUE TO STAY ACTIVE BY WORKING LATER IN LIFE.

31.2% Aged 65–69

20.2% Aged 70–74

8.4% Aged 75+

Data from the Employee Benefit Research Institute report "Labor Force Participation Rates by Age and Gender and the Age and Gender Composition of the U.S. Civilian Labor Force and Adult Population," May 2018

Many people do work just for the pure joy of feeling productive, including a sizable portion of those in their Golden Years. If this is you, go for it. In today's gig economy, it is easier than ever to find a flexible schedule where you can feel independent yet stay fulfilled.

As you read the rest of this book and plan for your own financial future, keep the vision of your future financial independence in mind. It is this vision that will serve as your guide as you go about your daily walk. It will give a purpose for the thousands of financial decisions you make. Without a clear vision, you may feel aimless and lack a sense of purpose and clarity in how and why you deal with money. The vision acts as your motivation to do more and be more so you can put yourself in the best possible position to make it all come to fruition.

Chapter 2: Expenses Matter

When people think about planning for financial independence, they often think about their savings and investment strategy first. Savings is definitely an important piece of the puzzle. However, if you don't know how much money you are spending now or will need to spend later, your earnings and investment portfolio balance may not matter. Even before you think about saving more, you should begin to think about how much you spend now and will need later.

Consider this simplistic example. If a client came to me asking if $500,000 is enough to achieve financial independence and retire comfortably, my answer would be, "It depends." If you have a $500,000 portfolio and you spend $25,000 per year, then you would have a chance at success. On the other hand, if your expenses total $100,000 per year, it is likely that you would run out of money fairly quickly. *Your expenses matter*. Therefore, you need to place a price tag on your vision first. Later, we will return to the question of savings.

Are You Spending Too Much?

When clients do begin looking at their expenses, I find they have many questions. "Am I spending too much?" "How much should I spend on my house?" "Should I choose private school or public school for the kids?"

"How can I make a budget?" Or "I don't feel disciplined, so how can I monitor my expenses and save more?"

Often, new clients will come in and say, "Well, I know I'm spending too much." Yet they still aren't sure how to reduce the size of their monthly cash outlay or how to prioritize their monthly expenses. Before you can determine whether you're spending too much, you need to find out where your money is going by making a budget, or as I like to call it, your spending plan.

How Long Will It Last?

YOUR

$500,000

PORTFOLIO

WITH ANNUAL EXPENSES OF:

$25,000   VS. $100,000

COULD PROVIDE FOR SYSTEMATIC WITHDRAWALS FOR:

30+ YEARS   VS.   **5.6 YEARS**

**IN OTHER WORDS,
EXPENSES MATTER.**

ASSUMES A HYPOTHETICAL 5% ANNUAL RATE OF RETURN. THIS IS A HYPOTHETICAL EXAMPLE AND IS NOT REPRESENTATIVE OF ANY SPECIFIC INVESTMENT. YOUR RESULTS WILL VARY.

How Will You Determine Your Spending Plan?

You can make an annual spending plan, but I often find clients are more responsive to a monthly one. The question you need to answer is:

> Right now, what is it going to take for you to have the standard of living that you want in retirement, and what is it going to take for you to do the things from your vision that you are prioritizing in retirement?

It's important to be as detailed as possible. Ask yourself not only what the dollar amount will be for your living expenses, but also for travel, gifts to grandchildren, and donations to charity. When you get to this amount, examine it again.

Once you have a monthly price tag for your vision, you can begin to look at how your current budget compares. I find it best to think about sorting your expenses into three buckets:

- Necessary fixed expenses
- Discretionary lifestyle expenses
- Other discretionary expenses

Your necessary fixed expenses include the basics, such as power, water, gas, food, and shelter. You will have to have all of those, because they are all fixed expenses. Next comes your discretionary expenses. I have found that there are two very different kinds of discretionary expenses. The question for these expenses comes down to this: What are you prioritizing?

What Will You Prioritize?

Part of determining your budget and managing your expenses will come down to deciding what matters most to you in terms of where you are spending your money. There are discretionary expenses that you could live without, but you would hope you wouldn't have to do without. And then there are those expenses you don't necessarily prioritize or don't feel strong-

ly about, but your money is going there anyways. These other discretionary expenses are one of the best places to start cutting back. As a planner, I have found that these priorities can be very personal. What matters to one person may not matter to another. It's all a question of what you prioritize.

For example, you don't necessarily have to eat out. Your kids don't necessarily have to go to private school. And you don't necessarily have to travel. Yet for some of my clients, these kinds of discretionary expenses are very important lifestyle choices. Some people choose to pay for private school or invest a lot in their kids' activities because it is important for their family. For others, a frequent schedule of weekend getaways is important because of their strenuous careers and their need for a good work–life balance.

Then there are things that we all do that are inefficient. We all spend money where we don't really need to. So, when those things happen, the question you should ask yourself is: How much do you want to allocate to those expenses that aren't really on your priority list? Ideally, you would reduce the amount you spend on such discretionary expenses and put that money to better use, either by building up savings or paying down debt. However, the first step is to decide on your spending plan, prioritize your expenses, and see if your plan is workable.

Can You Live on Your Spending Plan Goal?

As you work to achieve your own financial independence, you may find that it's one thing to set a spending plan limit and that it's a different ballgame to live within it. Therefore, I will often suggest to my clients that once they get to an acceptable price tag for their desired lifestyle, that they consider living on this amount for 3–5 years prior to the official retirement date.

For many people, this can be a challenge, since their spending plan goal amount is likely less than the current amount they are spending monthly. This can mean a big reduction in their cash outlay for ongoing expenses. A lot of people planning to retire in 2–3 years will hear this suggestion and say, "I can't do that right now." And this illustrates an important point. If you can't do it now, you're not going to be able to do it 2–3 years, either. You have to get yourself in shape to do it.

There are many lessons that living on your ideal budget can teach you. You may learn the budget amount you have decided on is too low, and that your desired lifestyle will actually cost you more. I tell prospective clients all the time the best time to learn this is years before your desired retirement date.

If you do find that your spending plan goal amount is not enough to give you the life you desire, you have a number of options. You may choose to change your monthly expense goal, determine if you can save more, or push your retirement date back a few years. Another possibility is to treat your spending goal like you are training for a marathon.

For example, let's say you have five years before you wish to retire and

GET IN SHAPE FOR YOUR SPENDING PLAN GOAL

TRAIN TO LIVE WITHIN YOUR SPENDING PLAN GOAL
LIKE YOU WOULD TRAIN TO RUN A MARATHON

YEARS TO RETIREMENT	MONTHLY INCOME	MONTHLY CASH OUTLAY	MONTHLY CASH SAVINGS
FIVE	$8,500	$8,000	$500
FOUR	$8,500	$7,500	$1,000
THREE	$8,500	$7,000	$1,500
TWO	$8,500	$6,500	$2,000
ONE	$8,500	$6,000	$2,500
RETIRE		$5,500 GOAL MET	TOTAL ADDITIONAL CASH SAVINGS $90,000

THIS IS A HYPOTHETICAL EXAMPLE AND
IS NOT REPRESENTATIVE OF ANY SPECIFIC
INVESTMENT. YOUR RESULTS WILL VARY.

your ideal spending plan goal is $5,500 per month, but you currently spend $8,000 per month. You can work on reducing your cash outlay little by little instead of all at once. If your income is $8,500 per month, five years prior to retirement, you can put $8,000 in one operating checking account each month. Don't spend more than you place in this operating account. Instead, reduce expenses and discipline yourself to live off that amount each month for one year. The next year, you can reduce it to $7,500.

The difference between your income and the amount deposited for expense in the first year is $500. Then it'll be $1,000, and so on. Each year, you should place this monthly difference in your cash reserve savings or investments. Or use it to pay down debt. The goal in this exercise is for you to get your monthly cash outlay right-sized. Setting a spending plan that meets the needs of your standard of living will help you prove to yourself that you can live in your desired lifestyle, while also helping you reduce debt, build a stronger cash reserves position, and/or provide additional assets to create additional income to support you when you no longer work.

What About Your Mortgage?

Another key expense question I get is "Should I payoff my mortgage prior to retirement?" For many people, purchasing a home is one of the biggest expenses they will have in their lives. It makes sense to focus on how much you spend on a mortgage.

From my observations, the answer to whether you should pay off your mortgage is "It depends." Now, don't get me wrong. It's very rare for it to be a terrible decision for someone to pay off their home; more times than not, having no mortgage payment is a great thing. However, there are several situations where having a modest mortgage payment, as a percentage of your income, could be beneficial.

These are a few of the situations where I have seen a mortgage actually assist retirement:

- You have a very favorable, low mortgage interest rate.
- You have a pension or other fixed income sources available.
- Your mortgage payment plus all your other living expenses do not cause an excessive withdrawal rate from your investment portfolio. (See Chapter 5 for more information about withdrawal rates.)
- There are potential tax benefits. With recent tax law changes, tax benefits may not exist for some families. Consult your tax advisor to see if your mortgage interest would provide you tax benefits.

Situations where paying off your mortgage is something to strongly consider:

- Your mortgage payments are large, accounting for more than 50% of your monthly fixed income.

- You have a modestly sized investment portfolio, so paying off your mortgage could place less of a strain on your income-producing assets, while helping keep your distributions below the excess withdrawal rate.

- You are an ultra-conservative investor and saver. Individuals who fall in this category typically enjoy the comfort of not having a mortgage. They may also have a less aggressive portfolio strategy with a lower return potential, which means it is less likely that carrying a mortgage will benefit them.

If you are considering whether you should pay off your mortgage, I suggest you sit down with a professional and review your financial projec-

Monte Carlo Simulation

A Monte Carlo simulation is a probability model planners can use to understand the impact of risk and uncertainty in financial planning. A Monte Carlo simulator can help you visualize many of the potential outcomes of an investment decision so that you can better assess the risk of that decision.

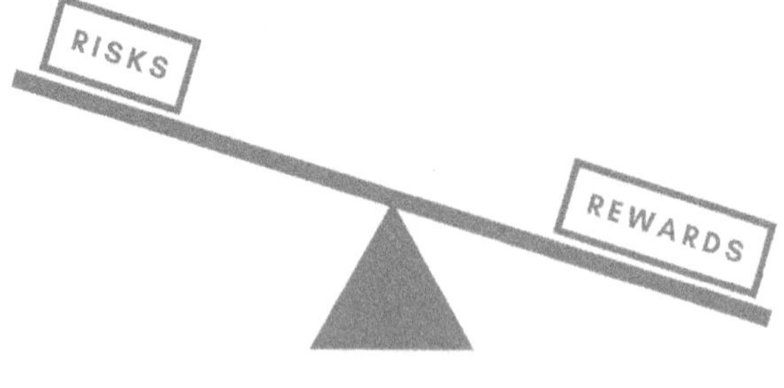

tions and a Monte Carlo simulation* to determine what might be best for your own particular case.

Other Expense Dos and Don'ts

Beyond prioritizing your spending, determining a budget goal, and reducing your cash outlay, there are several other "dos and don'ts" when it comes to expenses. Whether you are working to become financially independent or looking forward to your upcoming retirement, it is imperative that you not put off the task of preparing to manage your expenses. Waiting can be detrimental.

One of the most important "must dos" is to develop an affordable spending plan. Track it monthly and reevaluate it at least every six months. Also, make it a priority to eliminate unsecured debt. While there can be some benefits of carrying a mortgage in retirement, there is no case where carrying unsecured debt balances helps you live a more comfortable retirement. Many people will use their credit cards to earn reward points or cash back. However, this practice is only encouraged if you pay off the balance in full each month.

In terms of "don'ts," one of the biggest mistakes I have seen is to overspend. Remember that every dollar you spend is a dollar that you haven't invested in becoming financially independent and that you haven't saved for a rainy day. This situation can have a particularly big impact when it involves the purchase of a home. I always advise clients not to be "house-rich" and "cash-poor," because buying too much house often results in expense creep from hidden costs. You could find yourself in a situation where you've got

---

Note: While Monte Carlo results offer some reasonable estimates of likely outcomes, they do not represent forecasts, nor are any simulated results certain or guaranteed. Investment decisions should never be based solely on Monte Carlo simulations, since no Monte Carlo model can cover all the risks a client needs to consider (e.g., behavioral risk, inflation or health care risk, risk of living longer than projections, etc.). The use of Monte Carlo calculations requires a truly long-term perspective (10-plus years) as investor experience during any shorter individual periods can be strongly at odds with the long-term recommendations and outcomes of the model. Please be aware that the potential for loss (or gain) may be grater than demonstrated in Monte Carlo simulations.

to have the best landscaping and nicer furniture, utilities cost more, repairs cost more, and property taxes and insurance are higher. And yet that home and those expenses aren't part of your vision and your priorities.

Another issue with overspending on a house is that it can put you in a position to be unprepared for unexpected extraordinary expenses. I had clients that didn't listen and overspent on homes before the Great Recession. Then when they experienced an income disruption and their home values fell, it was a very difficult situation.

However, it's important to remember that in most people's lives, there will be rough patches where expenses exceed the ideal amount that allows them to live comfortably and preserve their assets. You have to think ahead and ask yourself, "What if that happened? What would I do?" That is why you should consistently spend less than you make. Whether those unexpected expenses involve your health, your grandkids' education, taking care of an elderly parent or relative, or unexpected travel, you don't want to have built a lifestyle that means you can't sustain yourself through that storm. Instead, please make sure you consider the unexpected so that you can see yourself through a rough patch by prioritizing the right expenses and knowing where your money is going.

Chapter 3: Cash on Hand

So you've worked your butt off to get your expenses in line in your quest for your financial independence, and you have now built up excess cash. The question many people have at this point is, "What do I do with all this cash?" My answer, in many cases, is just to leave it as cash. This is because the benefit of having cash on hand is found in having it *on hand* for those situations where and when you need it.

Why Cash Is King

As a planner, I have observed that financial independence is about more than just growing your assets to a specific dollar amount. It's also about the peace of mind, the reduction in stress, and the improved health and happiness that financial independence brings to people. Your cash reserves play a very big role in how you feel as you go about your walk through life. This is why having healthy cash reserves is one of my "must dos" if you want to achieve a comfortable retirement and gain your own financial independence. It's why I emphasize the mantra that "cash is king" when it comes to financial planning.

Cash reserves give people the sense that they will be okay. They know that if unexpected expenses or opportunities arise, they have the ability to address them and remain comfortable. A cash reserve is an important buffer to have, whether business or personal.

Imagine that your wealth is built in business, real estate, an investment portfolio, or retirement accounts. In the case of a sudden emergency, liquidating such assets quickly could have negative consequences. For your real estate or investment portfolio, your need could arise at a time when there are few buyers or when prices are depressed. Additional withdrawals from your retirement accounts could place you in a substantially higher tax bracket. And your business could need the cash to operate, and so it may not be available for withdrawal.

In any of these cases, "cash is king." It is readily available and accessible to handle those needs. When I counsel my clients about their cash reserves, I discuss how having cash comforts individuals, and also how many major U.S. corporations, who are earning cash hand-over-fist, have held a significant amount of cash since the dot-com bust, the 9/11 tragedy, and the 2008 financial crisis. These companies have kept cash on hand for stability. Just as it does for corporations, cash can bring individuals a great deal of peace of mind at all stages of life. This is especially true when your desired working years are complete.

Cash and Peace of Mind

One factor I have seen again and again for those preparing for retirement is that the clients who feel less stressed are the ones who have achieved a personally comfortable cash level. These clients typically have nearly a year's worth of expenses saved in case of emergencies or unexpected expenses. This is true even for clients who have a sizable net worth and retirement assets.

I have clients that have a net worth of $3–5 million dollars and others may have only $300,000–$500,000 as far as retirement assets, and yet it is those who *also* have a year's worth of cash on hand, no matter the size of their portfolio, that feel the most comfortable. Our meetings have a whole different tenor, and the way they approach their retirement goals is different, too.

I have other clients that have a couple million dollars in retirement accounts or business assets, yet haven't saved up a lot of cash, and they often tell me that they feel like they don't have anything. They can get stressed about potential emergencies or unexpected expenses and say, "Gosh, what's going to happen to us?" They don't have cash saved and so they feel worried, despite robust investment portfolios. That tells you the importance of having cash on hand from an emotional standpoint and how that tends to lead to peace of mind.

Putting a Price on Your P.O.M.

As with many areas of financial planning, decisions have a *benefit*, and they also have a *cost*. When it comes to the topic of cash on hand, people will often ask, "What interest rate am I earning on my cash?" And really, in today's world, cash is paying a very low interest rate. For comparison, a long-term growth and income investment portfolio could receive a 5–6% rate of re-

The Benefits of Peace of Mind (P.O.M.) Can Include...

- ☑ LESS STRESS
- ☑ BETTER HEALTH
- ☑ LONGER LIFE
- ☑ MORE ENJOYMENT IN LIFE

turn. Thus there is an opportunity cost for maintaining cash on hand.

In terms of interest on your cash reserves, I like to think of it like this: You try to earn as much as you can, but what you really earn for having cash is P.O.M. — peace of mind. That relief of knowing that you have what you need to take care of those unexpected events in life makes you less stressed, which, as we will discuss in future chapters, could mean better health. And better health has a positive impact on future expenses, on your longevity, and on your enjoyment and quality of life.

So, while maintaining cash reserves could "cost" you, in terms of that lost opportunity to earn some amount of interest, what you I believe you *will* earn is peace of mind, affording you some of those other benefits later on.

When it comes to working with my clients, I talk about having appropriate cash reserves. Any time we have excess cash, we do look at the interest rate it's earning. But at the same time, I will ask my clients, "Can you put a dollar amount on the peace of mind that it's earning?"

What About Your Own Cash Reserves?

If you haven't already built up your own cash reserves or emergency fund, now is the time to start, because it's never too soon to start earning P.O.M. as you work toward your own financial independence.

As I begin discussing this topic with clients, we generally take several factors into account:

1. What are your expenses? We need to know this figure first in order to establish the number you are comfortable with having in cash.

2. How stable is your income? Is your income made up of salary, Social Security, pension, or annuity income? Or is it totally from commission, your business, or an invested equity-based portfolio? The stability of your income is a big factor in how much cash on hand is needed.

3. Do you have excess dollars to achieve your retirement goal? After

a financial analysis and projection, do you show a strong probability of success without including the amount set aside for reserves? If a portion of those dollars is needed to work in your portfolio for your retirement, then we must identify the amount needed for income production and the amount needed for reserves.

BUILDING YOUR CASH RESERVES

FACTORS AFFECTING YOUR CASH RESERVES:

- ☑ Expenses
- ☑ Income Stability
- ☑ Retirement Goals

HOW MUCH SHOULD YOU SAVE?

Workers	3–6 Months
Business Owners	6–12 Months
Retirees	12 Months

NOTE: THIS IS A GENERAL RULE OF THUMB BY WHICH TO LIVE. INDIVIDUAL RESULTS WILL VARY.

When you are in your accumulation stage of life, the rule of thumb is to have 3–6 months' worth of expenses set aside for unexpected emergencies. A business owner should possibly have as much as 6–12 months' worth. As discussed above, for those nearing the end of their working years, it is usually advisable to build reserves equal to a full year's worth of expenses.

How to Build Up Your Cash?

Typically, if you're trying to save up three months of expenses for an emergency, then you want to put one month in an operating account, such as your checking account, then have another month in your local savings account, and have another month in your money market account or certificate of deposit (CD), depending on how large those dollar amounts should be. There are other factors to consider, but a third, a third, a third is a good general approach if you are starting to save. And if you're trying to build up six months' worth of expenses, you can apply the same by-thirds approach for where to put those cash savings.

Why Automate Your Cash Strategy?

Thinking about *how* to build up your cash, my suggestion is to do so automatically. There are a few reasons I recommend doing it this way. To start, if you set aside your excess cash automatically, you won't have to think about it, which helps increase the likelihood of your success. Another reason I often recommend automating your savings strategy is that most people are natural "spenders," so it makes sense to give yourself less to spend.

Are You a Spender or Saver?

One underrated aspect of financial planning is that different people have different personalities in regards to how they handle money. A lot of times you have people come in that are natural "savers." Whether due to the way they were raised, the way their parents taught them about money, or what they observed in their own life experience, either negatively or positively. Some people just save.

However, saving doesn't come as naturally for others. If you are a spender, that's where the path becomes a little bit harder, because personality and behavior are difficult if not impossible to change. However, you can make small changes that can positively impact your behavior, such as giving yourself less money to spend each month by moving excess cash out of your primary operating account. Like automatic bill pay, automatic savings right off the top of your paycheck is a great convenience and it can help spenders meet their savings goals.

How Much Are You Saving?

One of the challenges of achieving financial independence in today's world is that many people are natural spenders, not savers. For example, there are more people who walk into a store and make impulse purchases than walk into a bank and spontaneously save for enjoyment purposes. Generally speaking, we aren't saving as much as we should.

While some natural savers may be saving as much as 15–20% of their income each month in their savings account and 401k, others may lag behind in their saving goals. According to the Bureau of Economic Analysis, the annual U.S. personal saving rate has hovered between 6–8% the last several years after declining for the last several decades.

However, you should be saving more if you hope to achieve your own financial independence. During your accumulation years, even spenders

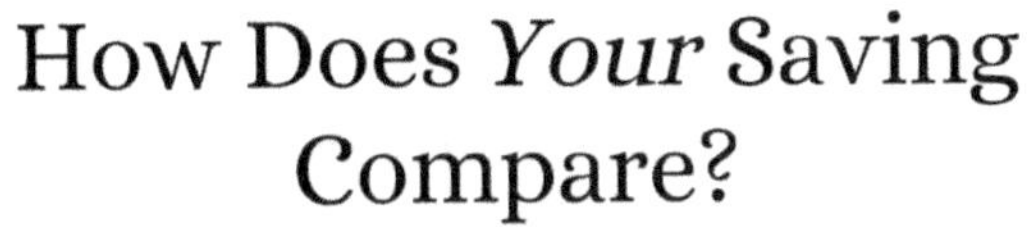

How Does *Your* Saving Compare?

THE U.S. PERSONAL SAVING RATE HAS DECLINED
OVER THE LAST 40 YEARS AND REMAINS WELL BELOW
THE 10-15% MINIMUM SAVERS SHOULD AIM FOR.

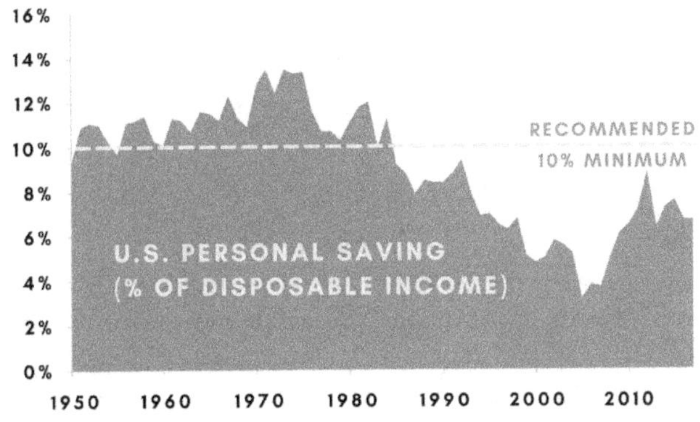

Data from the Bureau of Economic Analysis, "National Income and Product Accounts Tables," December 2018.

should aim to direct a minimum of 10–15% of their money to a savings account, 401k, or other parts of their investments. My very best clients save 20–30% toward all of their financial goals. Doing so automatically can help you reach your cash on hand goals faster, so that you can move on to growing your other investments.

Other Benefits of Cash on Hand

In today's world, cash is still king, and having an appropriate amount can positively impact your P.O.M. However, cash carries other benefits that works to help you achieve financial independence.

I have observed that clients with the desired amount of cash on hand have an easier time managing their investment portfolios, during both the accumulation and distribution phases. It's yet another underrated benefit of planning ahead for your cash reserves.

During the distribution stage, adequate cash reserves help ensure that you can maintain consistent and planned withdrawals from your investment portfolios. I have seen unexpected expenses during the distribution stage impact even the most disciplined budgets. Yet with an appropriate level of cash, clients rarely need to take excess withdrawals. Thus, the cash acts as an important buffer, giving you a better chance of having a lasting portfolio.

Additionally, I have found that having substantial cash reserves often correlates with more investment portfolio discipline during the accumulation stage. Clients with cash appear to be more comfortable accepting risk and withstanding downside volatility. In your accumulation years, a higher tolerance for risk and volatility may give you a higher probability of long-term success.

Most experts will tell you that investment success typically comes from "time in the market" vs. "timing the market." In my experience, having excess cash appears to give many investors the emotional strength to stay in the market and make better decisions for long-term success.

Chapter 4: Asset Size and Location

Clients often ask questions like "How much do I need to have saved to retire?" Or "What's my number (i.e., goal amount) in portfolio assets?" While these are very good questions, the answer is always different. Many people don't realize the importance of measuring the size of the portfolio needed in relationship to their goals. Often, they also forget that where they save their assets greatly impacts their growth rate and thus their retirement. Remember, it's your vision of your own future financial independence that should be guiding everything you do, including how large you grow your assets and where you keep them.

About Asset Size

What's your ideal investment portfolio size for your retirement? Say it with me now: "It depends." As I wrote in Chapter 2, your planned expense level is a major factor. I have worked with clients who were school teachers or dental assistants who have retired comfortably with less than or barely six figures of retirement savings. On the other hand, I have met with physicians and attorneys who have several million dollars banked for retirement, yet find that it will be nearly impossible to retire in the lifestyle they have built.

Modests, Extravagants, *and* Just Rights

If you have pensions, modest expenses, a paid-off mortgage, and reasonably good health, I have found that your investable assets can be very modest, and yet — so long as you have discipline and good fortune — you can live comfortably in retirement on smaller investment portfolio balances. On the other hand, if your expenses are large, your only source of fixed income is social security, you have parent or children obligations, and your health is not the best, then the size of your investment portfolio is an important key for you being able to retire comfortably.

The former group — let's call them the *Modests* — typically will have $100,000–$250,000 saved. These *Modests* may also have a pension which covers about 75–80% of their living expenses, and either have their mortgage paid off or will have it paid off in the first 2–3 years of retirement. Usually when we run an analysis on clients in this group, we find that they won't need to take withdrawals from their portfolio until much later in their retirement years. Their stable pension (or other guaranteed) income and modest expenses serves them well, even with their more modest asset size.

The next group — let's call them the *Extravagants* — might have $500,000–$2,000,000 plus saved. Their issue is not the size of their assets, but rather the standard of living they desire. Unfortunately, many clients who fall into the *Extravagants* category have not prepared as well for expenses in retirement. They have balances on their mortgages that will last through most of their retirement years. They have no pensions, which means that their investment portfolio becomes the main source of income to support the lifestyle they desire. Therefore, while *Extravagants* have a much larger asset balance then the *Modests*, their portfolios have to work much harder, which may put additional risks and stresses on their retirement goals.

I have found there is a third category of clients — let's call them the *Just Rights* — whose asset level often is well over the $2,000,000 mark. For the *Just Rights*, a comfortable retirement is usually defined by making smart life choices and decisions. They usually have more flexibility to choose their preferred standard of living. While *Just Rights* are not out of the woods when it comes to risks, this group has more flexibility built into their retirement.

Thus, it is true that you don't need $1,000,000 to retire comfortably.

But it is also true that you may need to build up several million in assets to maintain the standard of living you currently enjoy. This contradiction really comes back to the very important question of your expenses. High expenses will make it difficult for you to retire no matter how much money you have been able to save. It is the people who take the time now to develop a spending plan to reduce their cash outlay and maximize their savings potential that will be best positioned to enjoy a comfortable retirement and achieve financial independence.

About Asset Location

No matter the size of your assets, it is important to make sure that they are working for you to the greatest extent possible. Once you have developed a vision of what you are trying to achieve, prioritized your spending, and started saving, it is time to look at where you are putting that money.

Often, I have observed that much more attention is paid to the amount of dollars saved than the location of those retirement savings. However, asset location is very important. It could be the difference between retiring as a *Modest* or retiring as a *Just Right*.

As you work toward your financial independence, you should consider whether your investment assets are liquid or illiquid and whether they are pre-tax, tax-deferred, after-tax, tax-free or taxable assets. Also, you must evaluate your business and real estate assets. Can you turn those into an income stream or liquidate for profits? Why does each matter?

Liquidity

Consider liquidity. Assets can be either liquid or illiquid. Liquid is defined as an asset or savings instrument that can be liquidated into cash within 1–14 days. Savings accounts, stocks, bonds, and mutual funds fit this mold. However, homes, real estate, and business interests are often illiquid. It could take months to sell and convert these assets into cash.

Where you have built your net worth is very significant to how you manage your retirement. The more liquid you are, the more capable you are of dealing with emergencies or life events that require large amounts of

What's Your NET WORTH?

Net worth is a measure of your assets — such as cash, investments, cars, real estate, etc. — minus your liabilities — debts such as your auto loans, student debt, credit cards, and mortgage. It's a key indicator of your financial health, so it's important to work towards increasing your net worth by growing your assets and reducing liabilities.

cash to address. By having liquidity, your assets tend to be more marketable and the asset value more quantifiable. With liquid assets, you tend to know where you stand in value of those assets on a daily basis, which aids in understanding your capacity to better address the majority of life events.

Taxes

Taxes are another underrated issue that can really impact your retirement. For taxable investments — such as pre-tax, tax-deferred, or after-tax investments — the timing of when you pay tax is an important factor. Some investments, such as 401k contributions, are pre-tax savings that are tax-deferred, which means they will be taxable on distribution. With investments such as a Roth IRA or Roth 401k, typically you will pay tax on income you earn now and use to invest, but under current tax law, you will not pay taxes on the distributions you take after you are 59.5. One investment location is not necessarily better than the other in terms of tax. It all depends on other variables, such as your age, income, deductions, and other investments.

PRE-TAX, TAX-DEFERRED INVESTMENTS: 401K

I have observed that many families have the vast majority of their retirement savings in an employer-sponsored plan, such as a 401k. In my view, these are very necessary investments, but it's important to understand the tax implications. In a 401k, you are saving before-tax dollars. Those dollars potentially grow tax-deferred and, after the age of 59.5, you can withdraw those dollars without penalty, but taxes must be paid on distributions.

Over the last 40 years, as employers have reduced the number of pensions offered, they have provided workers access to 401ks to help them prepare for retirement. This has given workers access to the stock market and the ability to develop wealth through their place of employment. Unfortunately, many don't take full advantage of this tool, and those that do often don't grow significant investments outside of their employer plan.

AFTER-TAX INVESTMENTS: ROTH IRA

It is great to have a sizable 401k balance. However, workers should seek to balance this with other investment instruments. Roth IRAs and Roth 401ks are two options that are essentially tax-free when you take distributions in your retirement, because you prepay taxes on the savings you contribute to them.

The rule of thumb is to choose to save in a Roth IRA or Roth 401k when you are younger and your tax bracket is lower. The assumption behind that is that younger workers are in a lower tax bracket today and will benefit from taking withdrawals that are tax-free in the future, when their tax bracket may be higher. On the other hand, if you're an older, more established worker with higher income, you may opt for a before-tax 401k. However, for some workers, the Roth IRA could potentially allow them to pay less tax later when they are in their distribution stage and their tax bracket may be lower.

However, it's important to note that what works for most people doesn't work for everyone. I recently had a client who was focusing on building up his Roth IRA, though he is not young nor in a low tax bracket. He's a high-income earner who is 60 years old, but it's the right strategy for him because he has a sizable pension and will otherwise owe a lot of taxes when he retires and moves into the distribution stage. Using a Roth investment can help control his tax erosion down the road.

MIXING PRE-TAX, ROTH, AND TAXABLE ACCOUNTS

In many cases, it's advisable to use a mix of investments. Thinking about the issue of taxation helps illustrate this point. Consider how you might balance your employer's 401k plan and a tax-free Roth IRA — both of which we've already talked about — with a taxable investment portfolio.

Taxable investment accounts can be opened at most banks or financial institutions. In these accounts you can hold stocks, bonds, mutual funds, and/or ETFs. You save dollars you already paid taxes on in these accounts, and you pay taxes on dividends and interest each year or gains when you sell them.

By having this mix of investments, you can exert some control over your tax bill as a retiree. Consider these two scenarios:

You have $1,000,000 in a pre-tax retirement plan and no savings elsewhere. If you needed to withdraw $40,000 per year from your pre-tax 401k, your entire distribution is subject to taxation. Assuming a 25% marginal tax rate on those dollars, your taxes will be $10,000 on this distribution.

$40,000 (401k) × 25% = $10,000 Tax

On the other hand, if you have $600,000 in a pre-tax 401k plan, $200,000 in an investment account with a dividend yield of 4%, and $200,000 in your

> Roth IRA, and you spread your $40,000 withdrawal over those three locations, then your taxes may look like this:
>
> $24,000 (401k) × 25% = $6,000 Tax
> $8,000 (Dividend Income) × 15% = $1,200 Tax
> $8,000 (Roth IRA) × 0% = $0 Tax
>
> Your withdrawal is still $40,000 and your 401k distribution is still taxed at 25%, but because you have spread that withdrawal across a mix of taxable, pre-tax, and Roth IRA investments, your tax bill was lowered from $10,000 to only $7,200.

As you get closer to financial independence and retirement, it makes sense to look at where your assets are located because of tax erosion. Focusing on where you save is an important element to address.

Business and Real Estate Assets

Lastly, many clients have a significant portion of their assets located in what are potentially illiquid-equity assets, such as businesses or real estate investments. There are already more than 800,000 business owners in the U.S. over the age of 65, and with the current favorable business climate, I can see that trend is growing.

I have observed that these kinds of clients tend to be risk-takers with a full-fledged commitment to their business or real estate interests, which typically means that their business or real estate makes up a large percentage of their net worth. Throughout their working years, they may not have built up very many other investable assets, instead choosing to invest their resources in their business. They may also have a lack of commitment to other type of assets. Having so much of your assets in your business may have

Do You Own a Business?

OWNING A BUSINESS HAS GREAT POTENTIAL TO GENERATE INCOME-PRODUCING ASSETS NOW AND FOR YEARS TO COME. THE KEY IS IN UNLOCKING THIS VALUE.

THERE ARE MORE THAN

800,000

65+ BUSINESS OWNERS.

4% ARE OVER 70. **33%** ARE SOLE PROPRIETORS.

Sources: Guidant Financial and LendingClub. Small Business Study: Boomers in Business, November 2018. Shepherd, Lori. "Why an Increasing Number of Retiring Entrepreneurs Are Selling the Business to Their Employees." Entrepreneur, Feb. 21, 2018.

significant benefits, but it can oftentimes present major challenges when it comes to financial planning.

GETTING YOUR MONEY OVER THE FENCE

The most important question for these individuals is this: "Is your business producing income for your business, or for you personally?"

These two things are not the same, and if your answer is the former, you need to focus on developing a strategy for getting your money "over the fence." In the U.S., a high percentage of the wealthiest self-made individuals have made their wealth through real estate or business ownership, so there's no question that these can be very valuable and desirable assets. The challenge is figuring out how to unlock that value to enjoy a comfortable retirement.

Real Estate Assets

As a real estate owner, some strategies are very apparent. Many of these clients are able to turn their real estate investments into income-producing assets by receiving rental income that helps support their standard of living. This is typically the more conservative real estate strategy, since the potential price fluctuations in the underlying property values may not have much impact on the rental income.

Another strategy is "flipping," or buying undervalued properties, rehabbing them, and attempting to sell them at a profit. There is more risk to this strategy. Potential price fluctuations can leave this group of real estate investors in a bad position if their standard of living is dependent on those sales gains.

Ultimately, both of these groups most consider the cost of owning real estate, locating renters and buyers, the illiquid nature of real estate, and what percentage of their assets is allocated to their real estate interests. To counteract this risk, I have advised retirees with real estate assets to develop significant cash on hand and save in other types of investment accounts, as well.

Business Assets

Business owners have similar challenges. They spend their entire career building their business, investing the majority of their assets and company earnings back into the business. Typically, it's their passion and desire for independence that drives them to make the business successful. Yet often, their business's growth comes at the expense of building adequate retirement and investment assets. Therefore, the business owner must find ways to liquidate or transfer their business to unlock the value of their life's work for retirement. You can do so several ways.

The majority of businesses today are service-oriented. Likewise, a significant portion of Baby Boomer businesses provide professional services. For this kind of business, liquidating equipment and tangible assets often aren't options. Selling the business to employees, competitors, or children can be a good option. The clients I see who are most successful at this strategy often begin the conversation and planning for a sale 2–5 years in advance of their exit. Often, they will set up installment buyout programs that can last 3–5 years after their retirement.

I often challenge my business owner clients to develop strategies for their business to provide more passive income so that they don't have to be as active in their business. If you are a business owner, it is important that you build a business where you don't always work for *it*, but where the business will work for *you*. Ultimately, it needs to be an entity which will work well without your presence. This is when you will have a true business, and it's also when you will have a better ability to unlock the value for retirement income.

What Should *Your* Asset Size and Location Look Like?

So where should you start — as a *Modest*, *Extravagant*, or a *Just Right*? As I've already mentioned, there's no one asset size that should be your goal, and there's no one place to save your money, nor is there one right strategy for diversifying. It all depends. However, I have observed that there are patterns and strategies that generally work well for each category of client. Let's discuss each one.

The Modests

In my experience, this type of client often has a modest retirement plan (401k or 403b) from their working years. They also have pensions or other guaranteed streams of income. Oftentimes, their employer retirement plan is not their largest asset. They often have some cash savings, but they may have limited assets saved outside of their 401k.

If you fall into this group, it is very important for you to build the 6–12 months of cash reserves for liquidity. Because the vast majority of your income is coming from fixed sources, there is often no other way to address any emergencies than with cash on hand. It will be paramount for you to live within your means if you are a *Modest*. There will be no room for flexibility, as you will be on a fixed income.

Ideally, *Modests* should start off retirement with a cushion between the income they receive and their household expenses. This cushion will allow them to continue a modest savings program and help delay withdrawals on other savings or retirement plans until much later. That's important because a *Modest's* modest employer retirement plan can be very useful for warding off inflation as time goes on.

As time goes on, this cushion will disappear, not necessarily because the *Modests* are buying more things, but because their standard of living will cost more to maintain over time due to inflation. When this happens, it is important to have retirement assets positioned to provide additional income when it is needed. Often, this group may accept more volatile returns early on to battle inflation and later become more conservative as they use their assets for supplemental income.

The Extravagants

This type of client tends to have the majority of their assets in an employer retirement plan, such as a 401k. While they may also have a pension, it typically is not large enough to account for their expense level. So often, *Extravagants* will need to take significant distributions from their 401k early in their retirement years.

If you fall into this group, monitoring the volatility in your portfolio becomes very important. We have seen examples of extreme market downside volatility impacting a retiree's investment account in 2000–2002 and 2008, when retired individuals who had a significant amount of their retirement assets in equity investments saw a big decline in their investment accounts. Consequently, many had to reduce their retirement distributions.

The sequence-of-returns risk and rate-of-returns potential matters for these clients, since the majority of their retirement income is derived from equity assets in 401ks, IRAs, or non-qualified investment portfolios. If you depend on the income from your portfolios to cover living expenses, then volatility is an important area to manage.

Therefore, you should seek out income-producing assets if you are an *Extravagant.* Dividend-paying stocks, bonds, rental properties, and annuities are all options for you. While you will need growth as well, your first priority should be to understand what income is needed and then find income-producing assets to help cover that need as much as possible, with the growth of your portfolio as an important secondary goal.

The Just Rights

This type of client tends to want a mixture of growth and income within their portfolio. Typically their portfolio can provide a reasonable standard of living for themselves and their families. Volatility is important for this group as well, but it is a little easier to manage if they have a reasonable lifestyle, because they can place some dollars in a fairly conservative portfolio to cover their fixed and important discretionary expenses.

Then to satisfy their desired discretionary expenses and seek to add more growth, they can take more risk with the remainder of their assets. This helps the *Just Rights* meet additional financial goals, such as leaving an inheritance.

If you fall in this category, you have the ability to manage volatility in a more flexible manner geared toward your growth objectives. A mix of asset allocations often works very well for this group. You can use your income-producing assets to cover fixed costs and your non-income producing assets to help build a legacy and fight inflation.

Must Dos for Your Asset Size and Location

In summary, remember that it's not just saving that has an impact on your financial independence and retirement success. The decisions you make about the type of accounts and kind of assets you are building will also matter.

Realize that *Modests, Extravagants,* and *Just Rights* have different walks through life and through retirement, so the strategies each uses to manage their asset size and location will also differ. Note the different strategies. For *Modests,* it is extremely important to build cash reserves. For *Extravagants,* the focus is on the type of investment assets and keeping an eye on volatility. For *Just Rights,* the challenge is about balancing that risk/return trade-off as you ward off inflation and build a financial legacy.

Finally, I hope you will take away the lesson that your vision of financial independence doesn't have to cost a fortune. If you are disciplined and smart about your money now, you have a good chance of achieving your dream. On the other hand, a large pot of money won't necessarily guarantee success if it's not managed properly. Remember that getting disciplined about your spending and lifestyle choices now can lead to much better outcomes later, with less stress and more enjoyment. By keeping these factors in mind, you can maximize your chance of having a long and prosperous retirement.

Chapter 5: Income Distribution Strategy

You work all these years. You sacrifice and save. And before you know it, you are in your retirement. "How do I get income to live?" "How do I ensure I have income not only for today, but also as I get older?" These are questions I have heard very often as I help clients develop their income distribution strategy.

Developing a proper distribution strategy for your retirement is another "must do" if you are to have the best chance for a comfortable retirement. However, the importance of a distribution strategy is often misunderstood or ignored. I have found that a good understanding of this element can be very elusive for clients who don't have discipline or for people who don't seek out professional assistance.

The Cow and Its Milk Analogy

I like to give the analogy of the cow and its milk. I tell my clients at our initial meeting to think about their bucket of investments — whether employer retirement plans, 401ks, stocks, real estate, or other investments — and to picture these investments as their cow. I ask them to imagine a world where they need milk to live, and where milk alone is enough for them to remain healthy and happy for the rest of their life. I tell them that maybe they enjoy meat, and that meat is good in this world, but that milk is a necessity.

Luckily, they have the cow. They have raised the cow for years, feeding it and taking care of it, and now it can provide the milk they need to live, so long as they keep paying attention to its health. Its objective is to provide them with milk for the rest of their life.

On the other hand, they could decide that they want steak. If they start chopping the cow up for steak, it may survive for a little while, but if they keep eating meat from the cow, eventually they will kill the cow. The steak was great. But now, with no cow, they have no way to get the milk they need to survive.

The Cow and Its Milk

Think of your investments as your cow. Your cow can provide you a lifetime supply of milk. Or, it can give you a limited number of very nice steak dinners.

Don't Kill Your "Cow"

Killing the cow is a mistake I have seen again and again. It is how far too many deal with their investment portfolio. They need or want money, so they take larger distributions to make various purchases. Your ordinary distributions are the "milk" your investment "cow" can provide you. But when you start taking these larger distributions, you are no longer living off its milk. You are chopping steaks off your cow.

When you take more money in distributions than the investments can handle, you will begin to see your portfolio balance decline. I have often seen people come in and explain that their portfolio has dwindled and they need my help. In many of these cases, they have gained access to a pension or 401k investment in a lump sum. They wonder, "What happened to all my savings?"

The Lump-Sum Dilemma

In today's economy, downsizing and early retirement are common stories for those working for large companies. Such packages often involve a lump-sum pension and access to 401k funds. For others, retirement may not come early, but you still may find yourself suddenly staring at a very large investment balance of which you now have full access and control.

A person may work for most of their lives, earning $70,000, $80,000, or $100,000 per year, growing a pension over 25–30 years and saving in their 401k. Consequently, they may end up with, for example, $1.2 million that they have to roll over from those two accounts combined. Many have never dealt with access to that amount of money at once, and so they often do not take the right steps to properly care for their "cow."

The Mistake of Spending Down a Lump Sum

Often clients will tell me that they have taken large withdrawals to make large purchases or cover unexpected expenses and spent down their money. I have seen many examples where clients have splurged on an $80,000–$90,000 car, bought the fur coat they always wanted, or took care of other big-ticket expenses with money that was supposed to last them for decades. Aside from potentially jeopardizing their retirement, taking large unplanned distributions can also cause a tax increase, which only exacerbates the problem. Finally, your balance could also be hurt by volatility and taking a large distribution in a down market.

Fairly quickly, that $1.2 million could shrink to $700,000, which, in terms of a proper distribution strategy, can only produce a maximum investment income of $35,000 per year. Compare this to the $60,000 in maximum annual investment income the original lump sum of $1.2 million could have produced with a more disciplined distribution strategy. This example illustrates how difficult it may be to recover from a big shrinkage in your account balance. Your income, or "milk," must be reduced. Yet even with an income reduction, this situation often leads to people running out of money. They tend to repeat the cycle of taking these large distributions, and they kill their cow.

How Can You Protect Your Own Cow?

You may be wondering, "How do I avoid this? How do I not kill the cow that provides my milk — how do I protect the investments that provide my income?"

Get Professional Assistance

While no strategy can provide a complete guarantee, there are various types of investments that, when paired with a smart distribution strategy, can give you a higher probability of success. You can look at mutual funds, individual stocks, individual bonds, fixed annuities, immediate annuities, variable annuities, or a combination of all of these. We will not go into these various tools here, as you should be working with a respected professional to determine which one is right for you and your family. Nonetheless, I have seen each of these provide value to different clients based on their own personal situation.

Stay Within Your "Speed Limit"

Regardless of the type of investment you choose, it's key to stay within a certain "speed limit" for distributions. Large distributions, market volatility, and taxes can completely consume a sizable lump-sum investment in a matter of a few years, but it's important to recognize that the probability of running out of money is far lower for distributions that follow the speed limit. With the right distribution percentage, your retirement investment "cow" could remain healthy and happy for 25–30 plus years, and even outlive you.

The SAFEMAX Rate

In 1994, financial advisor William P. Bengen looked at more than 70 years of historic data for inflation and asset classes to determine the highest sustainable annual withdrawal rate for inflation-adjusted assets over a 30-year period. Bengen's purpose was to determine a conservative, *safe maximum rate* in a worst-case scenario. He later called this the **SAFEMAX Rate**, and pegged the figure at **4.15%** with a 50/50 allocation of stocks and bonds.

Bengen's research was published as "Determining Withdrawal Rates Using Historical Data," in the October 1994 issue of *Journal of Financial Planning*.

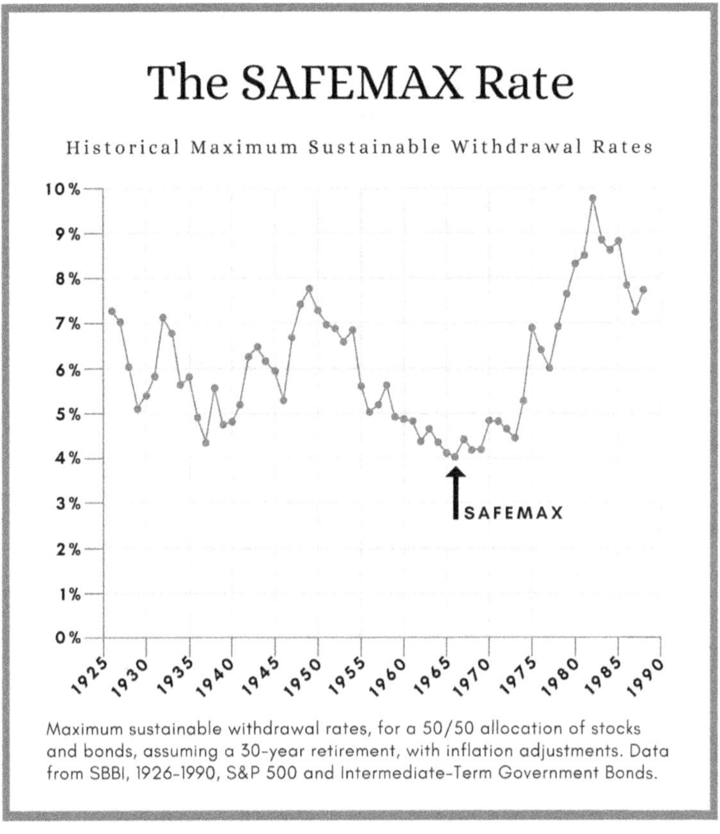

Maximum sustainable withdrawal rates, for a 50/50 allocation of stocks and bonds, assuming a 30-year retirement, with inflation adjustments. Data from SBBI, 1926-1990, S&P 500 and Intermediate-Term Government Bonds.

Financial experts have conducted a number of studies to try to determine what the ideal speed limit for distributions should be. Some have suggested that a speed limit as high as 7–8% can work. Others have put the limit at a very conservative 3%. However, influential studies suggest a withdrawal rate somewhere in between may offer a better return for a still acceptable level of risk. William P. Bengen suggested a safe maximum rate of 4.15% in his initial study. The Trinity Study, using similar methodology, found a rate of 4% to as high as 6% could offer a strong probability of success.

The 4-5% Rule of Thumb

FOR EVERY

$100,000

OF RETIREMENT SAVINGS

ANTICIPATE

$4,000–$5,000

OF RETIREMENT INCOME

	RETIREMENT SAVINGS		RETIREMENT INCOME
	$100,000		$4,000 – $5,000
	$250,000		$10,000 – $12,500
	$350,000		$14,000 – $17,500
4–5% X	$500,000	=	$20,000 – $25,000
	$700,000		$28,000 – $35,000
	$850,000		$34,000 – $42,500
	$1,000,000		$40,000 – $50,000

THIS IS FOR ILLUSTRATIVE PURPOSES ONLY AND IS NOT REPRESENTATIVE OF ANY SPECIFIC INVESTMENT. YOUR RESULTS WILL VARY.

Learn the 4–5% Rule of Thumb

Based on these studies and my own observations, clients who maintain a 4–5% distribution rate from their total investable assets have the highest probability of success in not running out of money. Therefore, as you consider your plan for retirement, you can start with a simple rule of thumb. For every $100,000 of retirement savings, you should anticipate it producing $4,000–$5,000 per year of income. The $5,000-per-$100,000 rule should be consider your maximum speed limit.

When you begin to exceed this speed limit amount, you may face eventual financial consequences. If you do it very often, then it is bound to get very costly, and it could end up costing you your cow.

In the context of your complete strategy, you will also need to consider additional factors, including your expenses, cash reserves, allocations, volatility, and other areas discussed throughout this book. The 4–5% rule can be very useful as you think about the before-tax income you are developing or accessing.

The Trinity Study

Another key piece of research into sustainable distribution rates was published in 1998 by Philip L. Cooley, Carl M. Hubbard, and Daniel T. Walz, who at the time were all professors at Trinity University in Texas. The Trinity Study, as it came to be known, followed the same methodology as Bengen, yet shifted focus from worst-case scenarios to portfolio success rates. The researchers noted that higher success rates correlated with lower withdrawal rates, shorter time horizons, and higher stock allocations.

The full Trinity Study, titled "Retirement Spending: Choosing a Sustainable Withdrawal Rate," was published in the February 1998 issue of the *Journal of the American Association of Individual Investors*.

THE TRINITY STUDY & RATES OF SUCCESS

HIGHER RATES OF SUCCESS CORRELATE WITH LOWER WITHDRAWAL RATES, SHORTER TIME HORIZONS, AND HIGHER STOCK ALLOCATIONS.

15-YEAR RETIREMENT HORIZON

W/D RATE	100% STOCKS	75% STOCKS	50% STOCKS
3%	100%	100%	100%
4%	100%	100%	100%
5%	100%	100%	100%
6%	89%	97%	100%
7%	80%	83%	84%
8%	71%	73%	72%
9%	68%	61%	52%
10%	56%	49%	37%

20-YEAR RETIREMENT HORIZON

W/D RATE	100% STOCKS	75% STOCKS	50% STOCKS
3%	100%	100%	100%
4%	100%	100%	100%
5%	91%	94%	99%
6%	81%	80%	79%
7%	71%	69%	61%
8%	63%	54%	41%
9%	50%	47%	29%
10%	41%	27%	6%

25-YEAR RETIREMENT HORIZON

W/D RATE	100% STOCKS	75% STOCKS	50% STOCKS
3%	100%	100%	100%
4%	98%	100%	100%
5%	82%	83%	85%
6%	71%	68%	58%
7%	62%	57%	42%
8%	52%	45%	22%
9%	40%	28%	8%
10%	29%	12%	2%

Using Ibbotson's Stocks, Bonds, Bills, and Inflation Data 1926-2017, S&P 500 and Intermediate-Term Bonds.

THE TRINITY STUDY & RATES OF SUCCESS

HIGHER RATES OF SUCCESS CORRELATE WITH LOWER WITHDRAWAL RATES, SHORTER TIME HORIZONS, AND HIGHER STOCK ALLOCATIONS.

30-YEAR RETIREMENT HORIZON

W/D RATE	100% STOCKS	75% STOCKS	50% STOCKS
3%	100%	100%	100%
4%	93%	98%	100%
5%	77%	77%	68%
6%	65%	57%	43%
7%	53%	45%	22%
8%	40%	33%	10%
9%	35%	13%	2%
10%	22%	3%	0%

35-YEAR RETIREMENT HORIZON

W/D RATE	100% STOCKS	75% STOCKS	50% STOCKS
3%	100%	100%	100%
4%	91%	93%	56%
5%	75%	67%	31%
6%	56%	53%	4%
7%	49%	35%	0%
8%	33%	22%	0%
9%	24%	2%	0%
10%	11%	0%	0%

40-YEAR RETIREMENT HORIZON

W/D RATE	100% STOCKS	75% STOCKS	50% STOCKS
3%	100%	100%	100%
4%	88%	92%	86%
5%	68%	64%	42%
6%	52%	42%	16%
7%	36%	30%	0%
8%	30%	6%	0%
9%	22%	2%	0%
10%	10%	0%	0%

Using Ibbotson's Stocks, Bonds, Bills, and Inflation Data 1926-2017, S&P 500 and Intermediate-Term Bonds.

Consider Other Income Sources

As clients begin to calculate the speed limit for their own retirement investment savings, it becomes clear that other income sources may be needed. Even with $500,000 in your 401k, you are only looking at an annual distribution of $25,000. In today's world, that is not a lot of money.

This is why it is important to think about how your other income sources may help you stay in the 4–5% speed limit. Consider Social Security. Will you take it at 62? Your full retirement age? Age 70? Or some time in between?

If you will need a distribution rate from your retirement assets that is greater than 4–5% in order to cover your expenses, you may decide to take

SOCIAL SECURITY BENEFIT OPTIONS

WHEN CAN YOU CLAIM BENEFITS?

- ☑ Earliest: Age 62
- ☑ Full Retirement: Age 67*
- ☑ Latest: Age 70

THE LEVEL OF SOCIAL SECURITY BENEFITS
YOU CAN CLAIM IS PARTIALLY BASED ON
WHEN YOU BEGIN CLAIMING BENEFITS.

Age 62	Age 67	Age 70
$986[†]	$1,408	$1,746
30% Reduction	Full Benefits	24% Increase

*Full retirement age is 67 for those born after 1960. †Benefits levels shown reflect the average 2019 monthly benefit for workers, according to the Social Security Administration. Please note: This example is for illustrative purposes only and is not representative of any specific investment. Your results will vary.

Social Security benefits before you reach full retirement age, even though you will incur a reduction in that social security income by taking early benefits. On the other hand, those who can live off 4% or less of their retirement assets, are likely to wait until the full retirement age or even age 70 to begin Social Security, in order to maximize their benefits. The decision of when to take Social Security is a very personal one. You should consult a professional on your personal situation before you make this decision.

For those with other income sources, the same consideration should go into your decision. A monthly pension is another income source that may assist you in maintaining a lower withdrawal rate. You should consider what dollar amount is available, at what age these pension payments are available to you, if they have inflation increases, and if there are survivorship benefits. Each of these factors may impact your ability to stay within a 4–5% withdrawal range.

Prepare Your Strategy

You have worked for years to bring to fruition your vision of financial independence and a comfortable retirement. Make sure that you give yourself your best chance at success by properly managing your income distribution.

In order to make the best use of your retirement investments, you need to be prepared with a strategy, as well as have an understanding of how income distributions are supposed to work. Remember that your cow is meant to provide the milk you need for years to come. Your cow very well may outlive you, if you take good care of it. Avoid the large distributions that will turn your cow into a steak dinner, especially for purchases that were never part of your original vision.

Begin your planning by considering your own 4–5% distribution speed limit. Remember that cutting your expenses by developing and sticking to a disciplined spending plan can help you stay within your budget. And consider your other allocations and sources of income. Finally, don't be afraid of seeking out professional advice. A professional can assist you in developing a personalized strategy that is designed to keep you within the 4–5% distribution range to maintain a comfortable retirement.

Chapter 6: Asset Volatility

In the world of investments, clients are always looking for the return. This is very understandable. You invest to make money and get your investments to grow. The potential to achieve long-term growth is the main reason people place their money at risk, investing a larger portion of their portfolio in stocks and equities. Early on in your saving years, tolerating more risk may help you realize more reward potential in the future. However, with that potential for a greater return comes the risk of increased volatility.

As you endure up and down markets, your portfolio will likewise have its ups and downs. This volatility is a key component for strategies that maximize asset growth during accumulation years, but volatility remains an important factor once you are retired and financially independent, too. Volatility won't play the same role in your strategy when you are living off your investment income as it did when you were working and saving. For many, the key to gaining financial independence and achieving a comfortable retirement is to recognize and effectively manage the changing role volatility will play in your portfolio.

The Return Chase

In the earlier working and saving years, I have found that investors tend to be accumulators. They are looking to build assets. Thus investment profes-

What Is VOLATILITY?

Volatility is associated with dramatic swings, either up or down, in stock and equity prices and values. Less-volatile securities have fewer such dramatic shifts, resulting in less risk and more certainty about that security's performance. However, volatile instruments offer the potential to maximize returns, albeit with greater risk and uncertainty.

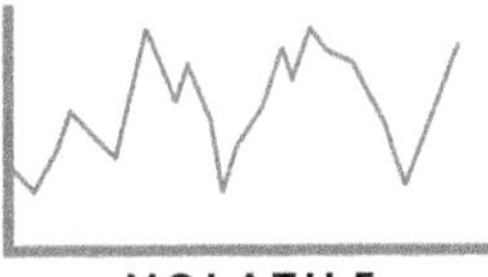

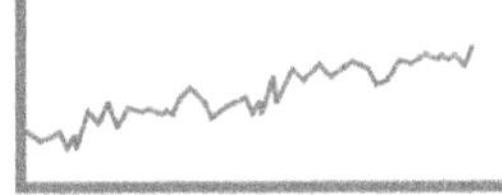

sionals tend to invest for them based on their risk tolerance and a long-term time frame. At this stage, risk has a lot of importance. The amount of risk the investor wishes to accept will relate to the volatility of their portfolio.

What Risks Will You Accept?

Like many aspects of financial planning, choosing your level of investment risk and volatility is a very personal decision. I often use the analogy of a roller-coaster ride to help illustrate this.

The level of risk an investor chooses is similar to what type of roller coaster they would select. Some people have a desire to get on a thrill-seeking ride, while some will choose a kiddie ride; still others choose something in between. Each type of roller-coaster ride will have different twist and turns.

Risk vs. Return

WHAT RIDE WILL YOU CHOOSE?

VOLATILITY CAN BE A FRIEND DURING YOUR ACCUMULATION YEARS. HOWEVER, AS YOU APPROACH YOUR FINANCIAL INDEPENDENCE, YOU MAY NEED TO REEVALUATE YOUR CHOICE OF ROLLER COASTER.

Just as you determine whether a roller-coaster ride will be a kiddie ride or a thrill-seeking ride before you decide whether to get on it, an investor should determine what type of risk they are willing to accept before they place their money in an investment. If they want a more exciting ride, they will invest more aggressively, which means having more equities and stocks in their portfolio. If they want a smoother ride, they will invest more conservatively, which means having more bonds and cash in their portfolio.

What Risk Means for Volatility

For an accumulator, volatility can be a friend. The more risk you take, the greater the potential for long-range returns. However, the ride along the way may be filled with several peaks and valleys. Investors may see their dollar value go lower in the down years.

Yet those same down years in the market can be a friend for accumulators. It allows them to purchase more shares at cheaper prices, thus assisting them in long-term asset building, as asset prices may recover and appreciate in the future.

However, as you approach or enter into your retirement, you may need to reevaluate your choice of roller coaster. This is because as one moves closer to retirement, portfolio risk and volatility become even more significant.

Repositioning for Income Production

The ride you choose matters in all investment years, but even more so as you approach and enter retirement. There are several reasons why this area needs to be evaluated closely.

To start, your primary focus should transition away from accumulation as you approach retirement. The key to your success will rest on being able to reposition your goal from accumulation to income production. Repositioning is key, because the volatility that may have been beneficial for asset growth in your accumulation years can become a major detriment to your long-term success in your retirement years. The reason for this is twofold. Your portfolio assets need to be able to reliably produce income for your annual distributions, which is difficult if the balance is shrinking due to volatility. Secondly, your time horizon to make up for any downward market volatility is much shorter, because you will need to take distributions soon. Consider this example:

> **You have a $100,000 retirement portfolio. Due to market volatility, your asset value drops 20% to $80,000. Following the 5% rule of thumb, you take a $5,000 distribution. Now your balance is $75,000.**

> A 20% portfolio decline and a 5% distribution will need a 33.33% return to get your portfolio back to its $100,000 value.
>
> Now consider a portfolio that declined not by 20%, but only by 8%. With all other factors being equal, then your $100,000 would have declined to $92,000. After your $5,000 withdrawal, its value would be at $87,000.
>
> In order to get your balance back to $100,000 the following year, your portfolio needs to have a return of 14.92%.
>
> While the 14.92% return is a difficult number to reach, it has a higher probability of happening than the 33%. It is very important for retirees to maintain principal for income-producing capability. Controlling the downside threat in your portfolio is a key to making that happen.

How Timing Affects the Distribution Stage

Over time, it becomes clear that it is not just the return on investment that matters. When you are in your distribution stage, it is also the *sequence* of successive returns that matters. There will always be up markets and down markets. However, it is important to realize that the timing of when you decide to retire may be impacted when you are exposed to downside exposure.

If the beginning of your retirement occurs during or just before a mar-

THE SEQUENCE OF RETURNS

THERE WILL ALWAYS BE UP MARKETS AND DOWN MARKETS, BUT TIMING MATTERS. IF YOU ENTER YOUR DISTRIBUTION STAGE NEAR A MARKET DOWNTURN, IT CAN BE DIFFICULT TO RECOVER.

RETIRING IN AN UP MARKET

YEAR	YEAR-END VALUE	WITH-DRAWALS	RETURN
0	$100,000	N/A	N/A
1	$103,000	$5,000	8%
2	$109,330	$5,000	11%
3	$124,009	$5,000	18%
4	$136,371	$5,000	14%
5	$147,735	$5,000	12%
6	$156,031	$5,000	9%
7	$168,195	$5,000	11%
8	$178,332	$5,000	9%
9	$185,816	$5,000	7%
10	$190,106	$5,000	5%
11	$177,502	$5,000	-4%
12	$158,302	$5,000	-8%
13	$129,557	$5,000	-15%
14	$116,783	$5,000	-6%
15	$105,944	$5,000	-5%

AVERAGE RETURN = 4%

THIS IS FOR ILLUSTRATIVE PURPOSES ONLY AND IS NOT REPRESENTATIVE OF ANY SPECIFIC INVESTMENT. YOUR RESULTS WILL VARY.

ket downturn, it could have a much larger impact on your portfolio balance and make it difficult for you to recover, even when the market turns. Consider these two sequences of returns:

THE SEQUENCE OF RETURNS

THERE WILL ALWAYS BE UP MARKETS AND DOWN MARKETS, BUT TIMING MATTERS. IF YOU ENTER YOUR DISTRIBUTION STAGE NEAR A MARKET DOWNTURN, IT CAN BE DIFFICULT TO RECOVER.

RETIRING IN A DOWN MARKET

YEAR	YEAR-END VALUE	WITH-DRAWALS	RETURN
0	$100,000	N/A	N/A
1	$90,000	$5,000	-5%
2	$79,600	$5,000	-6%
3	$62,660	$5,000	-15%
4	$52,647	$5,000	-8%
5	$45,541	$5,000	-4%
6	$42,818	$5,000	5%
7	$40,816	$5,000	7%
8	$39,489	$5,000	9%
9	$38,833	$5,000	11%
10	$37,328	$5,000	9%
11	$36,807	$5,000	12%
12	$36,960	$5,000	14%
13	$38,613	$5,000	18%
14	$37,860	$5,000	11%
15	$35,889	$5,000	8%

AVERAGE RETURN = 4%

THIS IS FOR ILLUSTRATIVE PURPOSES ONLY AND IS NOT REPRESENTATIVE OF ANY SPECIFIC INVESTMENT. YOUR RESULTS WILL VARY.

Let's say that you retire and begin taking your portfolio distributions at the beginning of an up market. Over 15 years, you take your 5% annual distribution and see an average rate of return of 4%. A down market occurs near the end of this hypothetical example, but your early gains help to cushion your balance from the impact of the later downside years.

Now consider the outcome with the same $100,000 portfolio, the same 5% annual distributions, and the same 4% average rate of return, but with the sequence of returns reversed.

In this case, our hypothetical retiree was just beginning to take her distributions when the down-market volatility occurred. The impact of poor returns was much greater, even though the average return for both examples is 4%.

This is an important point I communicate to my clients about the beginning of an up-market retirement versus the beginning of a down-market retirement. The sequence of returns and how we manage that volatility really matters.

How Will You Manage Volatility?

The same volatility that was a friend in the accumulation stage can be a challenge in the distribution stage. But the answer isn't to get off the roller-coaster ride entirely. I have found that while many may look to invest aggressively, there are a significant number of extremely conservative investors who will accept very little volatility within their portfolio. This can be almost as dangerous as being too aggressive.

Invest to Manage Inflation

Even in the distribution stage, you need to invest aggressively enough to account for inflation as well as the distributions needed to support your lifestyle. If your annual distributions are 5% and inflation is 2%, you are losing 7% of your purchasing power each year, even before factoring in any returns or losses.

Consider the impact of investing in more conservative investments. Investing in CDs in the current market may give you 2%. A bond portfolio historically may yield around 4%. A person living off these investments may be fine, initially. However, over time, it is quite possible that you could see your account and purchasing power erode. This won't be due to a problem of exceeding your spending plan or not staying true to your lifestyle and vision. Conservative investors who run into these portfolio erosion problems typically aren't buying more stuff or doing more things. The erosion is due to cost-of-living increases, portfolio distributions, and low returns. The initial lifestyle you planned for in your accumulation years now simply costs more than it did a few years ago.

Strike a Balance With Risk and Reward

The question of what to do about volatility is not an easy one — volatility isn't all good or all bad. Instead it is a factor to be managed and balanced according to the goals of your investment strategy at a particular time. Volatility can be great when you are in your earning years and have a long-term investing strategy. It can also play an important role in your distribution years by helping you stay ahead of inflation and your withdrawals. But it is important to pay attention to your downside exposure in your later years. You don't have the benefit of a long investment horizon, and a declining value caused by being too aggressive may impact the money you need to support your income. It is a delicate balancing act, to say the least.

I help my clients strike a balance on their volatility exposure by determining the maximum amount of risk they are comfortable taking and what risk level is called for to give them the highest probability of success. Once we have done this, we can develop a strategy. We can determine an appropriate mix of foreign and domestic stocks, bonds, real estate, and other instruments to help them reach their goals.

Volatility is a key component to success or failure when it comes to gaining financial independence and achieving a comfortable retirement. How you manage this aspect of your strategy is just as critical as any piece of your financial plan.

Chapter 7: Contentment and Confidence

One of the most overlooked elements of financial planning is developing a sense of contentment in where you are in your life and in your finances. For many of us, contentment is an elusive feeling. Life brings many disruptions to our plans. It's not always — or even often — going to be smooth sailing when it comes to your family, health, marriage, finances, economy, or career path. At some point, life will throw you a curveball.

These challenges will often impact your financial plan. This is something we cannot control. However, how you handle such adversity can also impact your financial future, and your response to such challenges is something that is within your own control.

In my career, I have observed many of my clients face unexpected challenges and I have been privileged to see many persevere through tough times, demonstrating their own inner peace. What stands out to me about these individuals is their faith and their commitment to planning, despite life's ups and downs.

Faith

I have been very fortunate to work with many clients who are people of faith. Whether Christian, Jewish, Muslim, and other religions, I have found that most people tend to have a belief in something or someone who is greater than themselves. It is said that in the Christian Bible, finances are mentioned more than 800 times, supposedly more than any other topic. I think that God wanted to emphasize to us that there is a proper perspective and purpose for money. While we need it for quality of life on this Earth, money is not our source of contentment and comfort. Instead, I think faith can be a source of contentment and comfort when it comes to dealing with money, particularly during tough times.

Faith and Money During Tough Times

Here in the South, I grew up in the church where my father was a Baptist minister. Faith is a big part of my life walk and life journey and I often see it play out in my clients' lives as well.

Back in 2008, I had one client who was downsized from AT&T due to the recession. She had just purchased a home and soon saw her new home's value go down tremendously with the housing crisis. She was now out of the workforce and way underwater on her mortgage. She was leaning on her faith a lot, because things really didn't look very good for her financially. But she had taken a retirement package from her job and found a few things to do with her time. She worked at her church, not making a large salary, and she spent time doing volunteer work. She also continued to keep her faith and plan for her future.

It was tough for a while, but things did turn around. Eventually, she was able to refinance her home under President Obama's Home Affordable Refinance Program (HARP). That gave some relief. Soon, she was able to get a really great corporate job with one of the leading privately-held companies in the country. It's a growing faith-based company, and she has prospered there, with promotions and raises. She's now in a much better position than she was a decade ago — free of debt, building her cash reserves, managing expenses, and again thinking about her retirement.

As a financial planner, I have seen how this client and many others look inward during these difficult times. However, I have also seen many clients find peace in their faith when things are going well. In these circumstances, many people of faith look outward.

Faith and Money During Great Times

Faith not only keeps people steady in tough times — it also keeps them grounded in the great times. When things are going well, many people find a sense of peace by looking for ways to be a good steward, to be of service to others, or to surround themselves with people they love.

Stewardship

Many of my clients exhibit their faith not in words alone, but in how they treat others, such as their coworkers, employees, and customers, as well as in their giving. Many are generous contributors to charity with both their time and money.

Many of my clients understand their stewardship responsibilities when it comes to money. They know that the net worth we have helped them develop is not the source of their contentment. It becomes important for them to place finances in a proper perspective, which makes planning easier. They prepare as well as they can for difficulties and don't panic and get off track when life throws them the inevitable curveball. Having this faith is the ultimate security and peace. They understand that money is just a tool that the Higher Being provides them to live comfortably on this Earth.

Service

Zig Ziglar stated, "If you help enough people get what they want, you will get what you want." This attitude of service is another quality I have seen with many of my clients. They believe in serving others, feeling their life has a greater purpose than themselves.

I have seen many who feel their business or profession is their Gift, which inspires them to help their patients, clients, customers, students, or employees whom they serve generously with their skills, time, and resources. Many of these clients express a desire to continue serving others, even after they have achieved their own financial independence and have the ability to retire. For this group, service becomes a way of life that brings a sense of contentment that money alone cannot.

Another attitude among this group of clients is the desire to leave a legacy for their children and grandchildren. There's a motivation to save properly and preserve assets for their own use, as well as for the use of future generations. I have found this to be one of the strongest incentives to prepare for the future and stick to a long-range game plan. My clients will often look to their finances and see these sorts of goals and motivations that are greater than themselves.

Wherever you are in your own life path, I encourage you to think about what motivates you. If you are not sure what will bring you peace — if you have not yet found something to strive for that is greater than yourself — now would be a good time to reflect. I have found the motivations that lead to the peace that will carry you through good times and bad are very personal. Your own personality, beliefs, and life experiences will shape your own vision of peace and how you strive toward it.

Proper Planning

No matter your own vision and motivations for achieving financial independence and a comfortable retirement, it will be difficult to reach your goal without proper planning. It can be difficult to deal with the peaks and valleys along the way, and you will find that you'll have competing financial goals and interests. Remembering to make and stick to a plan will help provide a sense of confidence, whether in tough times or great times.

Planning and Confidence in Tough Times

Financial planning goes beyond plotting out investments and growing assets. I have observed that a financial planner can also be invaluable when life throws you a curveball. When that happens, seek out an accountability partner in a financial counselor who can give you objectivity, and can listen, understand, and help you develop a plan to get out of it. That unbiased outside perspective can steer you away from mistakes that might make your situation worse.

If you cannot always afford to hire a personal advisor, there are other options. Just be sure to find an accountability partner that is objective, unbiased, and looking out for your best interest.

Planning and Confidence in Great Times

I believe it is helpful to understand that there are peaks and valleys and that there is a greater hand that takes care of you so you can take care of others. I have a belief in God and Jesus Christ, so I have a specific faith, but I also want those who may not be in that faith walk to understand that these words are also relevant for them.

When you are planning during the great times and looking for that sense of peace, it's important to think about purpose. What is your purpose? What are you trying to plan for and why are you working to build your financial assets? Discovering a faith in your own purpose will lead to your motivation. That in turn will lead you to a sense of contentment and confidence in following your plan.

Planning and Peace and People

Finally, it is important to note one last element of contentment and confidence, which is to surround yourself with people who you love and who love and care for you. My dad always said, "You are who you hang around." This has been true in all of my walks of life, and I have observed this to be true in financial planning, as well. So, don't forget to plan for people.

I have seen many single clients get to their retirement and have no friends or very little family with whom they can enjoy traveling or spending quality time. Often, the people they know are not prepared for retirement, and so they cannot afford to do the same activities. Consequently, many of these clients struggle to schedule and do the things they wished, because they are not surrounded by those who are equally prepared.

On the other hand, I have had clients find their motivation and purpose to plan by observing their own friends and family. They see how their friends are preparing and so they prepare to make sure they are not left behind, working hard to save properly and making good decisions. In this case, it's not about "keeping up with the Joneses," but about being inspired to improve themselves.

We all need something in our lives to inspire us to greater things and bring us contentment and confidence in our life's work. Whether it is a faith in God, a commitment to stewardship and service, or surrounding ourselves with loving people that we can share life's precious moments with, it is this sense of purpose that will give you the motivation you need to prepare and gain a sense of peace for your financial future.

Chapter 8: Independent Children and Grandchildren

"How do you plan for your financial independence or your retirement when you have young children or young adults living at home?" This is a question I have heard often as a planner. From a financial perspective, children are an important variable that you must take into account. I have seen how mistakes with money when the children are young, when they are in college, when they are adults, and even when they start having children of their own can have a negative impact on the client's (i.e., parents') financial security. To avoid such setbacks, it's important to make a plan and stick to it, know what you're going to do about college, and do your best to ensure they become independent. But first, it's important to talk about what having a child today costs.

Financially, Kids Cost

Children are wonderful to have. They are a blessing and bring a tremendous amount of joy to our lives. Becoming a parent is a wonderful thing, and becoming a grandparent is arguably an even greater joy. But children can be a major financial challenge. When we are thinking about earnings, expenses, and savings, it is important to be objective about our kids. Financially, they cost.

THE COST TO RAISE A CHILD IN THE U.S.

$233,610

Average estimated cost per child for a family of 4 from birth to age 17 as of 2018, according to the USDA.

BUT WHAT ABOUT AFTER AGE 18?

Helping pay for college, spoiling the grandkids, and factoring in the lost or reduced earnings for parents away from work?

$1,800,000

A 2012 New York Times estimate factoring in half of a typical college education, lost or reduced earnings for a mother and/or father away from work, helping a child with expenses from age 18-25, and expenses for eventual grandkids, found the total cost of a child could clock in at nearly $2 million. Today, the figure could be even higher.

Sources: US Department of Agriculture: The Cost of Raising a Child, 2017. New York Times: The Cost, in Dollars, of Raising a Child, 2012.

By some estimates, each child that you have is the equivalent of almost $2 million of net worth. Even still, that analysis is based on them being independent by 25. But what if they are not?

Are You Over-Supporting Your Children?

In what I have observed as a planner and a parent, supporting a child financially from birth to age 25 is no easy task. However, most families can make an effort to plan for these expenses. It is more often the unplanned expenses for adult children past the age of 25 where bigger problems occur.

Planned Vs. Unplanned Support

Over-supporting children can cause many to-be retirees to fall short in their pursuit of a comfortable retirement and make it difficult to achieve financial independence. Today, many families face unforeseen financial burdens. The Sandwich Generation are those people, often in their 30s and 40s, taking care of young children as well as elderly parents at the same time. This alone can put a strain on their financial planning. And I have seen another trend of unplanned support that could be even more impactful. There are now a large number of people in or near their retirement who are taking care of elderly parents and *adult* children.

Young children need your care and support to make it to adulthood, and it is completely understandable to take care of elderly parents who are no longer as independent as they once were. However, you should proceed with caution when it comes to taking care of adult children who you were counting on becoming financially independent themselves.

When Support Becomes an Expense

Now don't get me wrong. As a parent myself, I completely understand the desire to provide support. Oftentimes, life will throw us and our children unexpected challenges where a little unanticipated support becomes a necessity. I have seen situations where my clients who are parents help their kids get a new start, enhance their career, or assist with small grandchildren. Often in these situations, the kids are working hard, making good decisions, and moving toward their own independence. In these cases, I'm in agreement when my client says, "That's what family is for."

But what if your child isn't moving toward their own independence? In my experience, parents should proceed with caution when taking care of kids who consistently make poor decisions or don't have a sense of drive towards independence. I have observed clients who are borderline with the security of their own retirement redirect many of their resources toward supporting their children and their children's families. When that support becomes an expense for the parent and not an investment in their child, the parents should reconsider the degree of support they are providing.

When the Kids Move Home

The trend of multiple generations living under one roof has been on the rise. In some cases, this has to do with some Americans' cultural norms. But for others, it is done out of necessity. It is important to develop a game plan with your family. Discuss your plan together and aim for a balance where no one family unit is overburdened financially.

Finally, understand that kids who aren't independent can impact your ability to reach your financial goals. Every person retiring or preparing to retire needs to assess their situation with their adult children. What dollar amount of assistance are you willing to provide monthly or yearly? If you are committed to this support, it must be accounted for in your living expenses. This will help you more accurately determine what assets and income are needed to support your goals as you support your children. More importantly, ask your adult child, "If I keep taking care of you, who is going to take care of me — or both of us — when I no longer am able?"

Struggle Is Where You Grow

I believe over-support happens because parents do not want to see their children struggle, even as they may have struggled themselves. We want our kids to be successful, and there's nothing wrong with investing in your child at any age to help them get there. But remember that struggle is where they grow. When you don't allow your child to struggle because you offer too much help or the wrong kind of help, you could be stunting their growth. This can create a cycle of dependence from which it is difficult to break free.

Are You Planning Enough for College?

Most people having a child today dream that their child will one day go off to college. It is often as big a milestone for the family as it is for the child attending the university. Yet in terms of finances, it is another area where the huge cost of raising a child is readily apparent, and another area where I have seen clients have difficulties if they are not prepared.

The fact is that paying for 100% of a college education is not affordable for most Americans today. According to the College Board, annual tuition

What's It Cost?

THE COST OF A COLLEGE EDUCATION IN 2019

$10,230
Public Four-Year Institution
Tuition and Fees for the
2018–2019 School Year

$35, 830
Private Four-Year Institution
Tuition and Fees for the
2018–2019 School Year

Source: The College Board, "Trends in College Pricing 2018 Report"

and fees for the 2018–2019 school year cost an average of $10,230 for a public four-year college and $35,830 for a private four-year college.

A college education is on track to cost even more in the future. Compared to 30 years ago, the average tuition and fees for a private college have more than doubled, and for a public college, more than tripled.

The growth rate of education costs is expected to continue to outpace the rate of inflation, which is something to keep in mind if your children are still young.

Planning Early

If you have a goal of achieving financial independence and a comfortable retirement and you have a child who will one day be college-bound, I would say that first and foremost, you should sit down with your partner and start

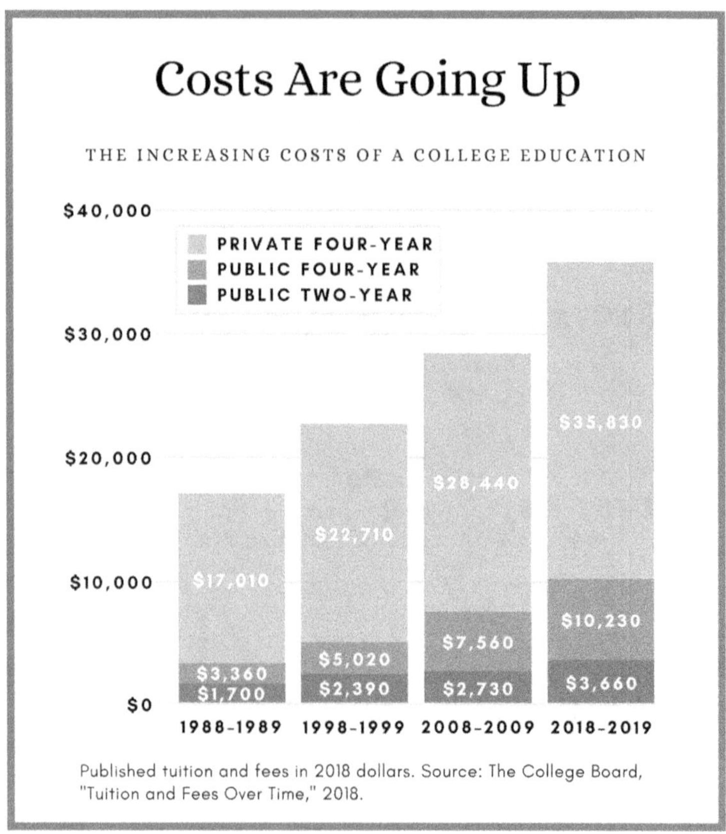

Published tuition and fees in 2018 dollars. Source: The College Board, "Tuition and Fees Over Time," 2018.

the discussion, the sooner the better. Determine what it is you want to be able to provide for your child in terms of educational support. Knowing that the full expense is likely to be more than you'll be able to afford, plan ahead for what portion you will pay for, then involve your child in the discussion.

I have clients who do different things. Some decide to pay for the first two years, some decide to pay for tuition and fees only. Others decide to pay for in-state tuition for a public college with the idea being that if the child decides to go to a more expensive private college, the child will know ahead of time that they need to fund the rest of the expense with scholarships, work study, or loans.

After you have determined what you will pay, you need to start saving for it, just as you would for cash reserves, your own retirement goals, and so forth. Decide how much you need to set aside and where you will save it. There are many options, from savings accounts, to savings bonds, a 529 plan, mutual funds, and even real estate investments. Each has its function, but you should evaluate each option carefully.

RETIREMENT SAVINGS

Having a kid in college during or just before retirement presents a challenge. In these years your spending plan will call for cutting back on expenses and your earnings will be winding down. If you use savings and assets earmarked for your own retirement to pay for college expenses, they won't be available later when you need them. Proper planning is the best way to address this issue, and my best-prepared clients are more likely to stay the correct course for retirement. However, if there are limited dedicated savings for education, parents often go to other sources.

First, they might use their retirement assets. This can be detrimental, since assets redirected to pay for the cost of education leave fewer assets to address retirement needs at an age where it's difficult to make up for those lost savings. Also, remember that most retirement assets are pre-tax savings. Upon withdrawal, the money is subject to income tax. If a parent takes out $35,000 from their IRA to cover a year of education, this amount is added to their income for that year. So, if you are in the marginal 35% federal and 5% state tax bracket, that withdrawal would be subject to $14,000 dollars in taxes. Alternatively, if that $35,000 was in a 529 college savings plan,* the withdrawal would incur $0 in taxes when used for a qualified educational expense.

Note: Prior to investing in a 529 plan investors should consider whether the investor's or designated beneficiary's home state offers any state tax or other state benefits such as financial aid, scholarship funds, and protection from creditors that are only available for investments in such state's qualified tuition program. Withdrawals used for qualified expenses are federally tax free. Tax treatment at the state level may vary. Please consult with your tax advisor before investing. Non-qualified withdrawals may result in federal income tax and a 10% federal tax penalty on earnings.

Paying for College

THE BEST COURSE WHEN IT COMES TO PAYING FOR COLLEGE IS TO DEVELOP A PLAN WELL IN ADVANCE AND STICK TO IT. A 529 COLLEGE SAVINGS PLAN ALLOWS FAMILIES TO PAY FOR COLLEGE WITHOUT DIPPING INTO THEIR OTHER RETIREMENT SAVINGS THAT MAY BE SUBJECT TO SIGNIFICANT TAX UPON WITHDRAWAL.

AMOUNT WITHDRAWN:

$35,000

PRE-TAX IRA		529 PLAN
TAX LIABILITY:		TAX LIABILITY:
$14,000	VS.	**$0**
35% FEDERAL PLUS 5% STATE		0% FOR QUALIFIED EDUCATIONAL EXPENSES

Note: This is for illustrative purposes only and is not representative of any specific investment. Your results will vary. Please speak with a tax or financial professional before taking any action.

CASH FLOW

Using cash flow to pay college expenses causes other problems. It's probably done by all parents, to an extent, but if the majority of tuition and books are covered through cash flow, the effects can be detrimental.

A rerouting of cash flow just before your retirement from retirement savings and other goals will impact your net worth. College education will benefit the child. They will potentially earn more money by having a degree, having an opportunity to increase their own net worth. But for the parent, all of the benefits are intrinsic.

Significant cash flow rerouted to pay for college will become a truly large expense item. The same dollars could have been used to pay down debt, save for retirement, or save for other life goals — all with the potential to grow your own net worth. I am certainly not advocating that parents choose these things over their child's education, but many parents fail to recognize that these choices impact their ultimate financial independence goal.

DEBT

Other issues can arise when you use debt, the least desirable of all of these options. Taking parent loans, 401k loans, or second mortgage loans are all debt options I have seen implemented. The immediate problem is that these options again reduce your net worth. The long-term problem is that cash flow will have to be diverted for a number of years to pay down that debt. These are significant reasons to not opt for going into debt to pay for your child's education.

OVERSPENDING

However you decide to fund your child's college education, please stick to your budget. It is important not to overspend. If you set a goal for an amount you will cover, *stick with it*.

On several occasions, I have had clients who were adamant that they wanted to pay for half, a lesser portion, or none of their child's college expenses. We based our long-term planning around this decision. Yet once the children were college-bound, these clients decided they needed to pay more than they had planned. I can tell you that this change of course resulted in those clients compromising on other priorities, such as their own financial stability and retirement. Reallocating a large amount of assets to a new education goal so close to retirement can put a prospective retiree's long-term security in jeopardy, because they typically do not have enough time to catch up on savings or realize a return to replace those dollars.

In order to avoid overspending and getting yourself into such a vulnerable position, be sure you set a realistic goal for what you as parents are comfortable providing for your child's education. It is important not only to think about what is financially comfortable, but also about what level of support will give you a sense of contentment and peace. Once you have set a goal, it's time to plan. Decide how much cash flow or other assets you will need to dedicate and where you will invest or save these dollars. A 529 plan, a Roth IRA, mutual funds, and savings accounts are all the options that I have seen work well.

What Will Your Legacy Be?

From my observation, grandparents tend to adore their grandchildren, maybe even more than their kids. As many parents do for their kids even after they are grown, grandparents want to help their grandchildren to have it better than they did. This is why the question of legacy is also important when you are planning for your financial independence. What will your legacy be for your grandchildren?

Many times, grandparents find themselves taking care of grandchildren. It's a joy to help, yet providing everything a grandchild needs on a daily basis can be very taxing and extremely challenging for the budget of someone facing or in retirement. If you think this might be a possibility with your own grandchildren, you'll need to account for the added expense in your retirement budget.

However, just because your grandchildren won't need you every day doesn't mean you won't want to help. In my experience, it's almost universal that grandparents want to help with what is extra, after the necessities are taken care of by parents. It is here that legacy planning comes in handy. Some want to help shoulder the cost burden for a college education. Some teach their grandchildren the family business or help them get a loan to start their own business. Others focus on leaving dollars after their passing. Proper estate planning and trusts are very important here. You'll need to determine what assets you don't need for living expenses and earmark those dollars for your grandchildren. You can create a will, add a trust, or use beneficiary designations or account titling to pass assets along to your grandchildren. Whatever your wishes and your desire to help, it is likely you will want to give your current or future grandchildren a leg up and help them have a great start in life. The best way to do so while sticking to your financial plan is to incorporate these goals into your plan from the beginning.

How Can You Help Them Be Successful?

For most people planning for financial independence and a comfortable retirement, children and grandchildren will be a part of the equation. They are a blessing and they bring much meaning and fulfillment to your life, but it is important not to ignore the cost of such blessings, so that you can plan for and maximize their chances for independence and success as adults.

The parents I know who have the most successful children have all done the same things to impart the importance of financial responsibility and independence. They give them chores around the house from a young age, teaching them that you are compensated for the things you do. They set a good level of expectation of the support they will provide, discuss college finances with them, and often, if they are able, give them a one-time push after college. Nothing is guaranteed in life, but with proper planning and the right habits, you and your children can position yourselves for the best chance at achieving your life and financial goals.

Chapter 9: Understanding Your Partner

While financial independence is a major life goal for many couples, it is still startling how many get divorced later in life. Almost 50% of all marriages end in divorce. "Gray divorce" — for those over 40 — is up, and one in four divorces are now initiated after age 50. While divorce is sometimes unavoidable, it is important to recognize that it holds the potential to ruin the financial health of all involved at any age. Real estate, pensions, retirement accounts, social security, college funds, and more can all be affected. There are nearly as many reasons for divorce as there are divorces. Yet in my observations, success in marriage is often correlated with success in financial planning.

Some say that issues within a marriage are a marriage issue and not a financial issue, but the connection is hard to ignore. Where such problems are lingering in a marriage, it will hinder a couple's financial growth, as well as their marriage. While it is true that some people do achieve a level of financial success despite strong marital disagreements, I wonder how much more successful they could have been had they been working together as a team. It could be the difference between running on four cylinders versus running on all six cylinders. If you are planning for ultimate financial independence, just know from my observations that the best teams are the most successful.

Divorce After 40

While divorce under 40 has dropped in recent years, "gray divorce" for those over age 40 is up, and divorce over 50 has doubled since 1990. It's worth pointing out that **1 in 4** divorces happens after age 50 and **1 in 10** are initiated after age 65. It's even common for these to be long-term marriages. About **34%** of these couples have been together at least 30 years. It is not uncommon for "gray divorce" to involve disagreements over finances.

Sources: Pew Research Center. "Led by Baby Boomers, Divorce Rates Climb for America's 50+ Population." Renee Stepler. March 9, 2017. The Council on Contemporary Families. "Gray Divorce: A Growing Risk Regardless of Class or Education." Susan L. Brown and I-Fen Lin (Bowling Green State University). October 8, 2014.

The Best Clients Are the Best Teams I Know

From my observations, my most successful clients with partners or spouses are those who excel at working together as a team. They don't always agree, but they work well together, and they respect each other's strengths and acknowledge their own weaknesses. They often define their own roles, whether they do everything together or one partner does everything, and then they stay in their lane. They have open and honest discussions about money and are aware that there will be times where they must agree to disagree or need to defer to their partner.

How you and your partner or spouse manage your money is incredibly important for your financial planning goals. There is really no single right or wrong way to do it. What matters most is that you have the conversation, learn to understand your partner, and decide on a game plan.

Your Game Plan

When it comes to developing a financial game plan with your partner, you will need to consider many of the same issues addressed elsewhere in this book — your vision, your cash reserves, your spending plan, your allocations, and asset volatility. Only this time, you will do so from a team perspective. In each case, you will need to get on the same page with your partner. Here are four questions to help you get there.

1. *Where Are Your Assets?*

Start with allocation. Where are you two accumulating your assets? The benefit of a partnership is that it is easy to diversify your portfolio allocations. Just make sure those allocations are part of a unified strategy.

Understanding your buckets of wealth creation as a family unit is critically important. You may have money in 401k plans, IRAs, your home equity, and other real estate investments or business ventures. The tax consequences for each will vary both in the accumulation stage and the distribution stage. Make sure you discuss how your current and future contributions can be coordinated to optimize your tax situation.

If you are building assets in real estate and business, then you need to ensure you and your partner are balancing this out with more liquid cash savings, for which the asset value can be readily assessed.

2. *Who Owns What?*

Ask yourselves, "How are our assets titled?" When there are two of you, it matters what names are on your accounts. In most cases, spouses and partners will begin to share expenses, debts, and other obligations together. Ask yourself which assets and accounts you own jointly. Oftentimes, if this is your first marriage or if few assets were accumulated during a previous marriage, then most or all of your assets may be titled jointly.

On the other hand, I have seen cases where one or both spouses were married before and have significant assets titled separately. Couples who get married after their careers have bloomed and savings are established are also likely to have more assets titled separately. Pensions and retirement plans are also individually titled, even if you're married. So how do you best handle these assets?

The most successful couples I have encountered in this regard excel at communication. They discuss all of their assets, held jointly and individually. They are aware of how their spouse intends to use these separately titled accounts and assets, and importantly, they are in agreement of titling, control, and plans.

I find this to be very important when doing planning, because savings and investment goals are set for a family, not individually. Therefore, even individually titled assets and accounts have to be taken into consideration for the family plan.

Communication is also important in the event of incapacitation or an untimely death. There could be a great financial hardship on the partner who has to locate, organize, and gain access to accounts of which they were unaware or that were titled separately with no access.

3. *How Do You Manage Day-to-Day Finances?*

Another challenge of working together with your partner toward a long-term financial goal is that you can lose sight of more immediate concerns. There are many ways to manage day-to-day finances, and there are no right or wrong answers. Still, someone has to be in charge of paying the bill that keeps the lights on, along with all of the other necessities of daily living. The married clients I have who are most in sync manage their dollars together, yet take on various roles. To determine who gets what role, they look at each other's strengths and weaknesses. Oftentimes, they find they can complement each other instead of living in conflict with each other.

4. *What Are Each Partner's Strengths?*

For every team there are different roles that need to be filled. In a business partnership, you'll often have a people person and an ideas person. In football, there is offense and defense. Each role has its place, and on great teams, each team member is ideally suited to their role. A marriage or partnership is not so different. Part of developing your game plan needs to be a discussion of how to maximize each partner's strengths. Then match the strength to the role.

THE MONEY MANAGER ROLE

Between you and your partner, who is better with money? Look at the situation as objectively as possible. Prior to marriage, who had the most savings, and why? Who made better financial decisions before you became a couple? Consider each partner's family history. Who was taught the best money management habits in childhood? Whichever person between you has the better track record should probably take the lead.

But what if you both are historically not good with money? This is not uncommon in today's world, with many people undereducated and underprepared to manage their family finances. If this describes your partnership, the answer is to start reading books together and educate yourselves about sound money management principles. Then, look for an accountability partner who can help keep both of you on track.

THE LONG-TERM PLANNER ROLE

Now look at which of you can fill another important role. Who is the better planner? Who tends to look more toward the future? Who considers the day-to-day in terms of how the present will impact your future plans? Who is the visionary? Who is the partner that dreams big and makes plans to get you both there?

The person with this strength should ideally take the lead for your long-term planning by shaping future goals while tracking progress and keeping the family focused on the big picture. This role and the day-to-day finance role tend to be distinct. One spouse or partner will feel more connected to one than the other and so the couple will each take one of these roles. Both are important. The day-to-day monitoring of finances is crucial, but so is looking toward the future with your goals, expectations and resources.

THE RISK-TAKER ROLE

Finally, one of the most important yet often forgotten personality types is one that a lot of couples tend to avoid discussing. Who is the risk-taker in your relationship? I'm not talking about who enjoys skydiving and bungee jumping. I'm thinking instead of two key traits necessary for financial success: entrepreneurship and risk tolerance.

Who is most likely to be entrepreneurial? Business and real estate are two of the most common assets owned by the wealthiest people in the country. For financial planning, being an entrepreneur can be a great thing.

What about risk tolerance? Who looks at potential big investments as an opportunity for a favorable return? For the family, the risk-taker role is very valuable. Oftentimes, risk-taking is dismissed as bad money management, and sometimes it is, especially when your financial foundation is weak. However, the role of the risk-taker within the family tends to be the reason for long-term financial success and stability. In terms of couples and money management, coming to an agreement over an acceptable level of risk is often one of the biggest conflicts I see.

Dealing With Conflict

Conflict is inevitable in all relationships. This is especially true when it comes to the subject of money. Realize that discussions involving money can bring up strong emotions for you and your spouse or partner. The way you were raised, your past experiences, and your attitudes all influence how you deal with money. It's unlikely that your partner shares all of those values and beliefs with you, which increases the potential for disagreement.

You Don't Always Have to Agree

As you plan with your partner toward a financial goal, it is likely you won't always see eye to eye. Disagreements over spending, saving, risk tolerance, and more will occur. The question is: What do you do about it?

First, understand that some level of conflict is natural. Everyone can strive towards an idea of the perfect team, but in reality, everyone has their own dysfunctions and idiosyncrasies. That's why it's important to know each other's strengths and weaknesses. Lean on the strengths and acknowledge the weaknesses.

Then try to bring the focus of the discussion back around to the goal. What are you trying to accomplish? If you can agree on the goal, you are halfway to resolving the conflict. All that is left once you have agreed on a goal is to find the best way to achieve it. Often an outside accountability partner, such as a planner or financial counselor, can be a great help guiding you and your partner through such discussions.

Seek Financial Counseling for Big Decisions

For big money decisions, major life changes, and other large money disagreements, the benefit of working with a financial counselor or planner can be invaluable. When my married clients are facing a big decision, finding the way forward is all about communication. A third party can help each partner understand the needs and emotions of the other partner as they face a big decision. They can also help keep the discussion focused on the important questions: What is the goal? Are we moving toward it? What is the best way to reach it?

Ideally, both partners can agree on a goal, commit to working toward it, and be open to compromising on how that goal can best be achieved so that both partners feel okay. In the case of risk-taking and asset volatility, I have often encountered clients where one partner is more conservative and needs to feel safe, while the other partner is a risk-taker and needs to feel understood. I say both need to feel respected.

The solution often involves each partner being given investor ownership over their 401k or IRA. They take responsibility to manage these dollars for those accounts, either more conservatively or more aggressively as they see fit. For other shared accounts and assets, they agree to a compromise that's not too conservative and not too aggressive. This can often appease both parties and keep disagreements from becoming a larger roadblock to success.

Practice a Level of Respect for Each Other

From my experience, you and your partner must come to an understanding on how you will manage your assets and work toward your goals if you are to be successful. Too often, problems within a partnership are ignored or dismissed, to the detriment of a relationship as well as the couple's financial health and stability. Left unresolved, disagreements over finances can lead to divorce, so it is important to make a plan, communicate, and realize you are both on the same team.

My very best clients practice a level of respect for each other's strengths, weaknesses, and differences that exemplifies this. From these clients, I rarely hear statements like, "You spend too much," or "You save too much." There's not any level of contempt. Instead, there is understanding. They approach these differences with a goal of listening, understanding, and meeting the needs of their partner as they work together toward their financial goals.

For those readers who are feeling frustration or even contempt over financial disagreements, I would tell them to seek out a marriage counselor so that they can resolve those issues. Even if the complaints are well founded, approaching your differences unproductively will be a hindrance to your success. Ultimately, you should strive to achieve a better level of respect and more patient communication, so that you can focus on the big picture and begin working together toward your financial goals.

Chapter 10: Good Health

So far, I have written about the importance of your vision, savings, investing, planning, family, marriage, children, and more. All are important pieces of the puzzle as you strive toward financial independence. Yet without good health, financial goals such as building assets and growing net worth will not matter very much.

My years as a planner have taught me that health is perhaps the most important aspect of our financial lives. Yet it often does not get the attention it deserves. This impacts not only whether we grow enough resources to become financially independent, but also — and more importantly — whether we are around long enough to enjoy the fruits of our labor. For this reason, I have saved the most important "must do" to close this book.

When planning for your future financial independence, you should plan for longevity and good health. Of course, you know that life may alter this plan at any point, and you could face unexpected health challenges. Still, we all hope for — and plan for — the best. Part of that plan should involve doing what you can to stay healthy so that you can enjoy the financial independence you achieve. So how do we take care of our mind and body? And how will this help with financial security?

Are You Being Intentional With Your Health?

In my observations, one way we can take better care of mind and body is by being intentional and making healthy lifestyle choices, just as we are intentional about how we manage our finances.

First, we should consider what happens when we are not intentional with our choices. Many of us have unorganized and busy lives, a dynamic that can manifest when we cram our lives with things which are not a priority for us. A busy, crammed weekly schedule may cause us to dine out more. We may buy more fast food for convenience, which studies have shown leads to a less healthy diet. An unhealthy diet oftentimes leads to more health issues, more doctor visits, more days not working, more missed opportunities for promotions and maximized earnings, and additional medication costs later in life. There's also the fact that eating out more can lead to a bloated monthly budget and possible overspending. When you cram your day too full of activities, you will find that you don't have the opportunity to organize your life, let alone your finances. But why do we lead such busy lives? How did our lives get so crammed?

It's not just our diets that can suffer when we have an unorganized and busy life. Work and family obligations can be necessary but draining, and when we become over-stretched, it can start to impact our mental health, which is such an important area of our lives, and yet we often ignore it.

As a planner, I have seen many clients attempt to cope with a busy and draining lifestyle instead of deciding to make healthier lifestyle choices. The method many use to cope is to "treat themselves" with trips to the mall, spa visits, or nights out on the town. Over time, this can have a significant financial impact. These expenses may soothe temporarily, but they may also blow your budget and make it difficult to build wealth, locking some people into what becomes a rat-race lifestyle. On the other end of the spectrum, some try to cope with alcohol or drugs, which can lead to addiction problems, divorce, and job turnover, tainting legacies and even destroying families. The emotional costs and financial ramifications can be severe.

In short, we don't just want to survive or cope with life. When we are not in a good place mentally, we are not living in our purpose and in our joy. It is just as important to be intentional about your health, about life, and about mind and spirit as it is to be intentional about your finances, because it all goes together.

What Health Choices Can Lead to Success?

Let's look at some tried-and-true practices from people who have learned to successfully balance their health with the rest of their lives. From my observations, these people are very intentional about health choices. Furthermore, my most successful clients all tend to be engaged in similar activities that not only benefit their finances, but their health and longevity as well. These clients have found that to run optimally, it's necessary to focus on five things:

- Getting exercise
- Watching your diet
- Seeking out counseling
- Taking vacations
- Watching your money

Let's take a look at each one.

Getting Exercise

From what I have seen, taking care of your body is the most important step you can take. My older clients in their mid-70s and beyond who keep moving are extremely happy. The sedentary clients are the least happy. In fact, this pattern tends to be true for my younger clients, as well.

Exercising can take many forms, from daily walking to the rigors of CrossFit. When it comes to lowering the risk of health problems, the physi-

Exercise and Mental Health

Evidence that staying active improves mental health is growing. Research shows that active populations have a **20-33%** lower incidence of depression.

Sources: Biddle, Stuart. "Physical Activity and Mental Health: Evidence Is Growing." *World Psychiatry*, June 2016. Dishman, R.K., Heath, G.W., Lee, I-M. *Physical Activity Epidemiology*, 2nd Edition. Champaign: Human Kinetics, 2013.

cal benefits of exercise are clear. Still, the mental health benefits also can't be overlooked. Find an activity that works for you, then keep moving for your longevity and your financial health.

Watching Your Diet

Along with exercise, it's important to watch what you eat. The goal is to take care of your body, so what you put in your body matters. I find that being intentional about having the best diet possible is a common trait of all my clients with good health.

It is no wonder that the wealthiest countries in the world have some of the longest life spans, while poorer countries have some of the worst life expectancy. One factor is that the diets are different. While it is true that it can be more expensive to have a better diet, this is often money well spent. A low-quality diet may be just as costly to your finances in the future due to negative health effects. A better idea is to reduce or eliminate unhealthy foods and increase your intake of very good food items.

Seeking Out Counseling (Spiritual, Secular, or Both)

For many people and cultures, counseling is still a taboo topic. However, from my perspective, both spiritual and secular counseling can be very effective tools for staying balanced, productive, and healthy.

Counseling and Your Health

COUNSELING MAY HELP MORE THAN YOUR MOOD; TAKING BETTER CARE OF YOUR MIND COULD HELP YOU LIVE A LONGER, HEALTHIER LIFE.

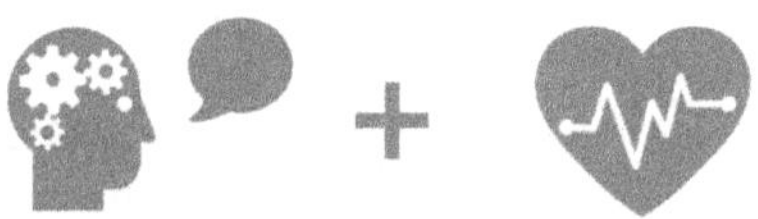

New research suggests that people with severe depression have a **53%** higher risk of cardiovascular disease and of those with cardiovascular disease, those with severe depression have an **85%** higher risk of death. Mental illness has also been linked to higher arthritis pain levels, more severe diabetes symptoms, and higher cancer mortality rates.

Sources: Correll, Christopher U. et al. "Prevalence, Incidence and Mortality from Cardiovascular Disease in Patients With Pooled and Specific Severe Mental Illness." World Psychiatry, December 2017. Lin, E. H. et al. "Effect of Improving Depression Care on Pain and Functional Outcomes Among Older Adults With Arthritis: A Randomized Controlled Trial." The Journal of the American Medical Association, November 2003. Scherrer, J.F. et al. "Increased Risk of Myocardial Infarction in Depressed Patients With Type 2 Diabetes." Diabetes Care, August 2011. Batty, G. David et al. "Psychological Distress in Relation to Site Specific Cancer Mortality." British Medical Journal, 2017.

The clients I have encountered who are most successful financially have a great sense of who they are, and they focus on building strong relationships with their partner. Often there is a deep religious belief which grounds them, or they are intentional about seeking out counsel when they need it. It is an investment of both time and money that can pay dividends for years to come. This is because balance and productivity more often lead to longer marriages, better careers, and a better overall quality of life.

Vacations and Your Health

GETTING AWAY FROM IT ALL, EVEN FOR A LITTLE WHILE, IS SURPRISINGLY IMPORTANT FOR LONG-TERM HEALTH.

For women, vacationing at least **2x** a year, as opposed to only rarely, reduces the risk of heart disease and heart attack by almost **8x**, according to researchers at Eaker Epidemiology Enterprises studying 20 years of data from the landmark Framingham Heart Study. For men at high risk of developing heart disease, taking frequent vacations can reduce the risk of dying from heart disease by **32%**, and of dying from any cause by **21%**, according to a 9-year study of 12,000 men sponsored by the National Institutes of Health's Heart, Lung, and Blood Institute.

Sources: Eaker Epidemiology Enterprises. "Myocardial Infarction and Coronary Death Among Women: Psychosocial Predictors from a 20-Year Follow-up of Women in the Framingham Study," *American Journal of Epidemiology*, 1992. University of Minnesota - Clinical and Translational Science Institute and the National Heart, Lung, and Blood Institute. "Multiple Risk Factor Intervention Trial: Risk Factor Changes and Mortality Results," *The Journal of the American Medical Association*, 1982.

Taking Vacations

Vacationing is necessary at every stage of life. Taking time for yourself and your family helps you get away from the stressors of the daily grind and may help you bond with your partner and children. Getting away from it all, even for a little while, is surprisingly important for long-term health. Multiple studies have shown that one or two weeks of vacation each year can significantly reduce your risk of heart disease, as well as all the associated costs that go along with it. Vacationing has likewise been shown to reduce the risk of an early death from other causes, as well.

When I sit down with clients, I always ask about their vacations and we work to help them plan and budget for time away from work. Although this is money that could have been saved, these are dollars well spent for quality of life. As a planner, the goal is for clients to have a long and full life. It's not about just waiting until age 65 to enjoy a vacation. It is important to balance your needs for both work and rest and to budget appropriately so that you can take enough vacation to maintain and improve your prospects for long-term health.

Watching Your Money

It is worth repeating that taking good care of your financial health will pay dividends for mind and body. My clients who make the smartest financial decisions — those who don't overspend, but instead build and maintain more-than-adequate cash reserves — tend to have less stress, more peace, and better overall health.

In a way, this brings us full-circle, because everything works together. Not spending more than you make and building a 3–6 month cash reserve not only helps you to feel financially secure, it is also a key component for mental and physical health. Money issues are one of the main causes of stress for individuals and families. Relieve the anxiety by saving instead of spending. Remember that "cash is king," and that when the money is going well, everything else tends to feel a little better.

How Health Can Impact Finances

Hopefully, as you are reading this, you will take my advice and do your best to be intentional about your own health so that you can have the best chance of enjoying a long and healthy life as you work toward your financial independence. I believe it is so important to close this book with the topic of health, because in my personal observations over the years, it always plays a large role in the lives of my clients.

I recall one experience particularly, when I was still fairly new to the financial planning profession. A new prospective client couple had come into the office for their first meeting. As usual, they had sent over all their information beforehand, so that I could review and be prepared for the meeting. They were older, in their early 70s.

Everything was going well and I remember we were having a great conversation. But as we began to go over their expenses, the man became very emotional. Tears filled his eyes. And I'll always remember what happened next.

I asked him, "Mr. Jones,* what's the problem?" And he said, "Well, you know all my life I worked hard, and I knew that when I retired, I wanted to have my mortgage paid off. I didn't want to have a mortgage at all. But now I'm retired, and I have a mortgage."

There was just one problem. When I reviewed the Joneses information before the meeting I did not recall seeing a mortgage! Now, I had only been a planner for a few years, but I knew that I was prepared for this meeting and as I looked at the paper again it was clear that the Joneses did not have a mortgage.

Finally, I asked, "Mr. Jones, you know, I'm sorry, but I don't see a mortgage here, so where's your mortgage?"

He looked across the table, put his finger on a line item, and said, "Right there."

His finger rested on a line item in their budget: medications for him and his wife at a cost of about $1,100 per month at that time.

---

* *Names have been changed to protect confidentiality.*

"That's my mortgage," Mr. Jones explained, "because we have to have it, and that's how much it costs. And I have to pay it just like I have to pay for someplace we need to live, so that we can stay well and can continue to function."

That meeting happened nearly two decades ago, and yet I've never forgotten it. It made a big impact on me as a young planner and it's something I think about every day with my current clients. The Joneses taught me an important lesson about health and finances. That meeting made me realize that there are some things we can plan for and some we cannot, and that we need to take every step we can now to control that which we can, including by taking care of our health.

When you are planning for your future financial independence, you've got to make sure that you are prepared for unexpected expenses that may come up down the road. The longer we live, the higher the likelihood that we will need costly medication or care to function and survive.

So you can't underestimate how much you are going to need in your retirement. Yet, what is within our control is how we take care of our mind, body, and spirit now, as we prepare for the future. So remember to take care of your health! As you plan for financial independence, do what you can to stay healthy so that you can enjoy the fruits of your labor.

Conclusion

In my time as a planner, I have found that different people have different reactions to discussing the 10 areas financial planning and wealth creation covered in this book. Some of you reading this may already feel energized and ready to begin planning for the life you want to live and your current or future financial independence. For those readers, I look forward to one day hearing how far your determination was able to take you.

I know that for other readers, the task ahead may seem daunting. Some of you may be worried about your current situation or about your ability to make the changes you need to make. For all readers, but especially those readers, I have one final observation to share.

On Perspective

It's true that it's not easy to become financially independent. If it was, everyone would do it, and I would not have a successful business. What I have observed in my years of being a financial planner is that some people experience adversity and let it stop them. Something doesn't go their way or doesn't work out as they expected, and as a result, they lose sight of their goal, they forget about the financial principles they've learned and get discouraged. They may even give up on their dream.

Now, it is absolutely true that there will be rough patches along the way, where life will hand you lemons you weren't expecting. But what you do have control over, and what I hope to leave you with here as we conclude *The Quest for Financial Independence*, is the importance of your perspective. How you look at the hand you've been dealt can be very impactful.

We all have those moments in our lives where we question the decisions we've made and the direction we're heading. "Man, I messed up there," "I wish I would've done that," or "I could have done this better." You may even have a time in your life when you think, "I'm failing."

I know that I had moments where I wondered, "Is this ever going to really happen?" I was wondering if I would be able to get to a point where I could help people working toward their dreams while also being able to take care of my own family in the way I had wanted. And as with other important moments in my life, with Kelvin Boston's *Smart Money Moves* and Stephen Covey's *7 Habits*, the answer came to me in the form of a book. Around the time of my darkest moments, I read John C. Maxwell's *Failing Forward: Turning Mistakes Into Stepping Stones for Success*.

Failing Forward was very impactful for me, because it forever changed my perspective. It helped me remember that failing is part of the journey. Even though we may not always execute as we intended, or we may not be at the place we think we should be, it doesn't matter so much, as long as we learn, persevere, and progress.

Financial planning is all about giving yourself the best probability of success. You can't do that if you let yourself get discouraged by the inevitable setbacks along the way. However, you can give yourself a much better probability of success by doing what successful people have done, which is learn, persevere, and progress. Consider focusing on the 10 areas of financial planning and wealth creation that I have discussed in this book, and plan forward.

Failing, Succeeding, and Planning Forward

One important observation I have had in this business is that there are always going to be bad times. My first 10 years as an advisor included the dot-com bust, 9/11, and the Great Recession. It was a hard time for many people, and yet all of us here got to the other side by persevering through that adversity.

This is because the principles I have discussed in this book work in bad times as well as the good times. I have been privileged to see many people work hard and persevere so that they can live the life they want to live.

Of all my long-term clients, there is one married couple that stands out. With several millions of dollars in assets and their dedication to planning for their financial future, they are on track to be very successful *Just Rights* in the years ahead. Truly, they are exceptional people.

However, if you had known them back when I first met them, some 15 years ago, you might not have noticed how exceptional they were. These clients have always been very smart, very dedicated to each other, very involved in their church, and they have always had a great outlook on life. But they have not always had a considerable net worth.

When I first met them, they were working with probably less than $100,000 in net worth. As I said, those years were not smooth sailing. They were just starting out. The dot-com bubble and the financial markets swings after 9/11 and many other not-so-big setbacks came to pass. Yet through it all, this couple stayed focused.

They continued to apply the principles discussed in this book, and to do so consistently. They remained dedicated to saving, cutting back on spending, building up their cash reserves, paying attention to asset location, monitoring volatility, taking care of their relationship and their family, and paying attention to their mental, spiritual, and physical wellbeing. They have heard the things I've written in this book ad nauseam.

Things didn't always go perfectly. They made mistakes, they faced their share of ups and downs from life, and yet they remained consistently focused on planning forward, whether they had just come from a failure or a success. Years later, their dedication has paid off. Today they are worth a few million dollars; but even upon reaching that major goal, they haven't lost focus on planning for their financial future and living the life they want to live.

Your Turn

In America, we have a tendency to compare ourselves to others when things aren't going so well, and sometimes even when they are going well. Even if we know such comparisons are unhelpful, it doesn't always stop us from thinking about it. The goal of this book is not for comparison's sake; but, for learning from others' success and gaining a new perspective. Don't recreate the wheel. Remember that the goal of financial independence is being able to live the life *you* want to live, and that this will mean different things for different people, because we each have our own vision we are working toward.

Now it's your turn. What is your vision for your future? Your answer can be whatever you want it to be. All that really matters is that you take what you've learned and start working toward it.

About the Author

Stanley T. Funches, CFP®, ChFC®, CRPC®, MBA, was born in Jackson, Mississippi, and raised in Clinton, Mississippi. He later went on to study finance and earn a BSM from Tulane University and an MBA from Samford University. Stanley began his journey in financial planning over 20 years ago, earning his Certified Financial Planner® Designation et al. During his time as a financial planner, Stanley has served professionals, business owners, and physicians as they prepare for and maintain a comfortable retirement.

Stanley has done numerous seminars and speaking engagements in his community and appeared on several news shows discussing financial planning topics. In 2001, he was awarded the Presidential Award by the Urban Financial Services Coalition. In 2007, he was profiled and labeled a "Wealth Pioneer" by Wealth Manager Magazine. In 2015, he was a contributing author to the Amazon Best Seller, *Voices of Inspiration — Real Life Wisdom for Living Your Best Life.*

Stanley is currently the owner of INTELUS Wealth Management, a financial planning firm which offers investments and financial planning services to those seeking to attain financial independence. Stanley resides in Birmingham, Alabama, and is the father of three wonderful children, Ashli, TJ and Christopher. In his time away from the office, Stanley enjoys basketball, golf, and reading.

www.ingramcontent.com/pod-product-compliance
Lightning Source LLC
Chambersburg PA
CBHW061743050726
47598CB00002B/567